A Practical Guide

THE EMPOWERED JOB SEARCH

Build a New Mindset and Get a Great Job in an Unpredictable World

CATHY WASSERMAN
&
LAUREN WEINSTEIN

Cover and Interior Design: Rebecca Pollock
Contributing Editors: Alieza Durana and Hannah Lindenbaum
Copyeditor: Jill Amack

Paperback ISBN: 978-0-578-90271-5

To A.K. Thank you so much for your pure
and beautiful love!
—Cathy

To Eli. Thank you for everything. You've made me a better
partner and writer!
—Lauren

Contents

Chapter 9
Make a Decision and Negotiate Your Offer

Chapter 10
Live the New Work Paradigm in Your Job

Introduction

Why Your Emotions and Mindset Matter Most

Looking for a new job can feel overwhelming and isolating. The experience plays on our innermost fears that we are inadequate, incompetent or don't belong. Many of us are conditioned to view work as a huge component of our identity and so looking for a job can feel like a moment of weakness. Your friends and family may even respond with pity: *"Sorry to hear that."*

It shouldn't be that way. We believe that the job search can be one of the most transformational learning experiences of your life. You get to dream big and imagine what's possible. In the process, you have the opportunity to develop healthy patterns of behavior that set you up to be successful and fulfilled at work.

Finding a great job should be easier than ever. Zip Recruiter's "Apply With One Tap" and "LinkedIn's "Easy Apply" make it seem quick and simple. Endless websites, apps and articles offer a stream of tips and tools to navigate the job search. Googling *how to put together a resume* yields more than 200 million results.

Despite technology making it easier than ever to apply, it still can feel daunting. Additionally, friends, colleagues and even career experts tend to give conflicting and confusing advice, leaving you wondering how to get started.

In *The Empowered Job Search*, our starting point isn't with cover letters or resumes, but YOU. We chose the title of this book because the job search can feel so *disempowering*. The hiring process is still heavily weighted in favor of employers' power and choice, not job seekers'. You might be one of many people who submitted a job application and even interviewed for a job, but never heard back.

In this book, we help you develop the psychological tools to build an *empowered mindset** to have the most agency in your search. Central to developing your mindset is connecting to your emotions at every stage of the process. When you step back and identify your feelings clearly at the outset, it's easier to identify a job that feels like a good fit and ultimately, save time and energy. Without doing so, you're more likely to fall back on "selling" yourself, diminishing your motivation and power.

The world we live in makes it difficult for many individuals and groups to fully live out their internal power because of systemic oppression. One of our main goals in writing this book is to humanize the job search, making the process as energizing and empowering as possible while also shifting broader power dynamics. So, when people in your life hear that you're looking for a new job, their instinctive reaction won't be pity or concern but rather curiosity or even inspiration. *"Wow, what a great opportunity, how can we help you?"* or *"I would love to hear more about what's next."*

We recognize that it's a privilege to identify what you want to do next. Not everyone has that opportunity. While we primarily focus on individual self-development, we're optimistic that some of what we write in the book can, over time, have a positive impact on rebalancing power in organizations and our larger culture.

The New Work Paradigm

This book calls for a new work paradigm in which we each take responsibility for our feelings and needs, while creating the space for others to do the same. We call this the virtuous cycle. This is especially important as many of us are addicted to work, technology, and social media, creating the illusion of more connection than there actually is. Pandemic fatigue has exacerbated the feeling of disconnection, even as many companies try to foster employee well-being and engagement.

---

* We define mindset as the conscious and unconscious thoughts, beliefs, feelings and needs that shape your ability to direct your outlook and experiences.

The pressure to succeed and be productive is only amplified by globalization, automation and artificial intelligence. Skills have shorter shelf lives; there's a need for ongoing learning, re-tooling and revamping expertise to keep up. As we write this book, there's a debate about what role remote work will play after COVID-19 and how our professional lives may be changed forever.

In the chart below, we outline five main principles of the new work paradigm. Self-awareness and emotional fluency underpin each. Organizations increasingly value these skills, and there's a growing understanding that they can't be replaced by new technology. We believe strongly that when more individuals and organizations embrace the new paradigm, we can build a more compassionate, creative and equitable job search experience and ultimately, workplace.

Old Paradigm	New Paradigm
You're passive in your approach and mindset. You don't prioritize your internal power in your work life.	You take responsibility for your power and proactively direct your work life. You recognize that you have the ability to develop an empowered mindset.
You dismiss or minimize your feelings and needs about what you want and what you think is possible for yourself.	You're able to identify your feelings and needs so that you know what you want and share more of who you are.
You spend a lot of time and energy hiding your perceived flaws. You don't see the importance of working with your vulnerabilities and their value in your work life.	You own your strengths and don't hide from your vulnerabilities, but rather find ways to work with them constructively and in some cases, transform them. You explore and claim the fullness of who you are.
You believe that in order to be successful, you need to be available 24/7 and hyper-productive, at times compromising your well-being.	You accept that you are a person with a wide variety of personal and professional needs. You integrate rest and rejuvenation into your daily life.
Your interactions tend to be transactional and self-focused. Conversely, you may neglect your own needs, focusing too much on others.	You prioritize balancing your feelings and needs with those of others, engaging in the flow of give and take. You advocate for both yourself and others, which has a ripple effect in the world.

Our Background and Approach

Cathy is a licensed social worker and has a background in leadership development, management consulting, community organizing, and mediation. Lauren is a management consultant turned learning and development professional, who, at the time of this book's publication, was pursuing her doctorate in organizational leadership and learning.

Our shared approach derives from more than thirty years as career and leadership coaches, working with thousands of clients across the public and private sectors at all stages of their professional journeys. We draw on insights from psychology, organizational development, leadership development and other related fields. While the book is based on our experience working with clients, we also share specific anecdotes from Lauren's job searches, as she went through two job transitions while writing this book.

Who This Book is For

The Empowered Job Search is meant for anyone who is looking for a new job or thinking about what's next. We hope the book is accessible for you, whether you're just beginning your professional journey or you're an established leader in your field. We share examples from different industries and sectors to expose you to a wide variety of positions and career options.

If you're reading this book, you're probably looking for a job with some meaning, or at the very least, something that builds on your strengths and better suits your needs and interests. We truly hope that you find something in this book that resonates with you and supports your self-discovery and learning!

How This Book is Structured

It's probably apparent by now that this is not your typical job search book. We go deep into the nuts and bolts of how to put together a compelling resume and cover letter, build your network, apply to jobs, interview, negotiate salary and much more, but we emphasize, above all else, how to maintain a healthy mindset and manage your emotions.

This book walks you through every step of the job search process, culminating with how to prepare for and be successful in your new job.

In *Chapter 1: Emotionally Prepare for Your Job Search,* we introduce you to common feelings, needs and beliefs that you'll likely encounter in your job search.

In *Chapter 2: The Emotional Breakthrough Process,* you'll learn our process for amplifying your positive emotions and dealing with difficult emotions as you navigate the job search.

In *Chapter 3: Set Up Your Search for Success,* you'll map out daily routines and structures to help you stay organized and motivated in your search.

In *Chapter 4: Own Your Unique Value,* you'll reflect on what makes you you—your unique value—and use it as a foundation to strengthen your application materials and interview preparation.

In *Chapter 5: Determine the Work You Want,* you'll clarify what you're looking for in your next job, including your must-haves and deal breakers.

In *Chapter 6: Community Building: More Than Networking,* you'll map your network and craft talking points to connect authentically with your community.

In *Chapter 7: Apply!,* you'll dive into the application process, from refining your résumé to writing cover letters, while discovering ways to manage your emotions.

In *Chapter 8: Get Ready for the Interview Process,* you'll prepare for interviews by getting into a positive and productive mindset, anticipating common interview questions, and following up.

In *Chapter 9: Make a Decision and Negotiate Your Offer*, you'll tap into your inner wisdom to make a thoughtful decision about whether to accept an offer, based on your must-haves and deal breakers.

In *Chapter 10: Live the New Work Paradigm in Your Job*, you'll take an empowered approach in your new job, and in the process create a more compassionate, creative, and equitable workplace.

Throughout the book, you'll develop strategies to deal with your emotions as they arise during the inevitable ups and downs of your search. Each chapter introduces a different mindset that's particularly useful for that step in the process and includes specific practices to help you get into that mindset. At the end of the chapter, we offer a "celebrate and maintain momentum" section so you can reflect and carry the momentum forward. We include stories of real job seekers and how they've navigated challenges using the tools in the book. (We've changed the names and personal details in these stories.)

While each chapter builds on the previous one, the process is certainly not linear. You'll likely want to come back to earlier chapters as you progress through the book, to remind yourself of foundational principles that will help you navigate your search. The exercises might feel like a lot to take in at times, so pace yourself, perhaps focusing on a chapter a week. And above all, do the exercises that feel most helpful to you or experiment with them and make them your own.

We're thrilled to share our joint creation with you! We hope that this book empowers you to get a great job, encourages you to build a better work world and inspires you to lead a happier and more fulfilled life.

Cathy and Lauren

Chapter 1

EMOTIONALLY PREPARE FOR YOUR JOB SEARCH

Get into a <u>PRESENT</u> mindset

Explore what's motivating you

Recognize your feelings

Identify your needs

Understand your beliefs

Celebrate and maintain momentum

Dionna
GETS
UNSTUCK

Dionna had been in her job as a research analyst for more than ten years and was feeling stuck. For one, she felt a sense of grief and disappointment that she had spent so much time in a position that never truly felt right for her. She sought Cathy out as a coach when she decided to get serious about finding a new job.

When they met, Cathy noticed that Dionna's instinct was to rush into editing her résumé as she was understandably anxious to apply for new jobs. But Dionna struggled to revise her résumé because she felt blocked and overwhelmed. Encouraged by Cathy's prompts, she started to explore her feelings and underlying needs and beliefs more fully instead of resisting them.

Before Dionna knew it, she was ready to tackle her résumé with much more focus and energy. She felt validated and more capable of getting into the details of her résumé. Using the strategies outlined in this chapter, Dionna realized that identifying her emotions was a critical component of her job search strategy.

Looking for a new job can unleash a tsunami of emotions. One day you might feel confident, ready to dive into your search, map out a plan, and make a to-do list. The next day, you might feel dread and confusion about where to start, whether or not you should tell your manager, or even if you should be looking for a new job. If you've been freelancing or out of the job market for a while, you may be unsure where to begin.

In this chapter, you'll get more comfortable naming and working with your feelings and underlying needs and beliefs. This, in turn, forms the foundation for building an empowered mindset that will help you stay motivated and propel your search.[1]

Recognizing your emotions and how to work with them[2] is essential to find a great job and ultimately be happy and successful at work.

UNPACK YOUR FEELINGS

Get into a 'present' mindset by unwrapping your feelings to reveal your deeper beliefs and needs

FEELINGS

BELIEFS   →   BELIEFS

NEEDS   NEEDS

---

1 Our approach is influenced by Marshall Rosenberg's NVC (Nonviolent Communication), Buddhist principles, and positive psychology.

2 For the sake of simplicity, note that we use the terms "feelings" and "emotions" interchangeably, even though there's a technical difference and much debate about these definitions. A feeling is a sensation, and everyone labels and interprets them differently. In comparison, an emotion is how we display a feeling out into the world; this may reflect our internal state and other times, it may not. Eric Shouse, "Feeling, Emotion, Affect," *M/C Journal*, 8(6) (2005), https://doi.org/10.5204/mcj.2443.

Get into a **<u>PRESENT</u>** Mindset

When you're present, you're more able to access your feelings, needs, and beliefs, allowing you to most fully experience yourself and the world. You're also able to focus on what is versus what was or what could be, helping you process what's directly in front of you. You then become more emotionally available and capable of making better decisions throughout your job search. A present mindset is the foundation for the other mindsets in the book, and you'll need it to do the deep work of connecting to your feelings and underlying needs and beliefs.

One of the fastest ways to get present is to take a few moments to pause and tune into specific noises or images around you. For example, you might note: *"There's an airplane overhead. The birds are chirping loudly."*

What do you notice about your internal experience and external environment that you might not have been tuned into before this moment?

_____

_____

_____

Explore What's Motivating You

Knowing *why* you want a change will help you to more deeply explore your feelings, needs, and beliefs. Review the chart on the next page and pay close attention to what resonates with you. Please note if you're experiencing more than one of these scenarios, which is common.

COMMON MOTIVATING FACTORS IN
THE JOB SEARCH

It's the right time for a change.	I left my job or I was laid off or furloughed.
I want to shift roles and/or sectors.	I don't know what I want.
I'm not doing the work I want to do or am meant to do.	A major shift in my personal life is making me rethink my career.
I don't feel supported at work.	I feel undervalued/ underpaid.
I want more meaning and purpose.	I'm overworked and burned out.

In order of priority, what do you think is motivating you in your search right now, even if it's not on this list?

1. _____

2. _____

3. _____

Recognize Your Feelings

We have seen repeatedly with clients that one of the best ways to enter the present moment and access your power is to get in touch with your feelings and find ways to work with them. This includes navigating difficult or negative emotions, as well as maximizing feel-good or positive emotions. The reality is that we can't turn off our feelings even if we want to.

HOW FEELINGS SHAPE YOUR JOB SEARCH

You're anxious about not having a job and feel compelled to take action. → You continuously apply to jobs, even though your approach is unfocused.

You're worried that you don't have enough experience for a specific position. → You decide you aren't going to apply.

You feel self-confident as you're prepping for a job interview. → You're likely to make a good impression and connect with the interviewer.

While there are almost an infinite number of feelings that can manifest in your job search, we've detailed the major emotions that our clients face. While many of our emotions happen simultaneously, we've separated feel-good emotions and difficult emotions, so that you can more easily identify what you're experiencing.

COMMON EMOTIONS IN THE JOB SEARCH

FEEL-GOOD EMOTIONS	DIFFICULT EMOTIONS
Joyful/Happy	Sad
Hopeful/Optimistic	Discouraged
Inspired	Frustrated
Peaceful	Anxious
Curious	Bored
Determined	Overwhelmed/Exhausted
Proud	Ashamed/Embarrassed
Celebratory	Angry
Energized/Excited	Isolated/Lonely
Confident/Certain	Self-Doubting/Confused

What emotions are most present for you right now, as you think about your job search? Note that your emotions may be in conflict with each other, and that's okay!

Identify Your Needs

We like to think of feelings as road signs that indicate whether we have met or unmet needs. Our needs are at the root of the feelings we experience. Imagine your feelings are inviting you to slow down to discover what you *truly* need.

Sometimes we inadvertently take on a loved-one's needs or those that seem desirable by society. For example, you may overemphasize salary to impress someone else or feel pressured to have a particular kind of job that you know is respected even if it's not interesting to you.

COMMON NEEDS IN THE JOB SEARCH

MONEY	I need a specific dollar amount to cover my basic living expenses.
STABILITY	I need a job with a good salary and benefits.
AUTONOMY/ FREEDOM	I need to decide how I spend my time and how I get my work done.
CONNECTION	I need to be part of a team.
MEANING	I need to find purpose in my work.
WELL-BEING	I need to stay emotionally and physically healthy.
SELF-EXPRESSION/ CREATIVITY	I need to be able to express myself through my work.
VALUE	I need to be acknowledged for my work.
ALIGNMENT	I need to do work that aligns with my values.
COMPETENCY	I need to excel at my job.
SOCIAL IMPACT	I need to contribute to the greater good.

What do you need most in your next job? Is this truly your need or someone else's?

_____

_____

_____

Understand Your Beliefs

Beliefs are shaped and internalized throughout our life. They play a major role in our self-perception and how we experience everything around us. Infinite factors shape our beliefs, which directly impact the job search, such as:

- **Your upbringing:** If a parent consistently told you that you're lazy, you may internalize that label and question whether you're truly capable.
- **Your experience:** If you've been fired a few times, you might understandably feel anxious about getting laid off.
- **Oppressive social systems:** If you've experienced discrimination based on race, gender, age, sexual orientation, class, ability, or other factors, it's undoubtedly influenced how you perceive yourself.

When you have a *limiting belief*—a way of thinking about yourself and the world that is rigid or absolute—it can be difficult to see nuance and/or possibility. You may sabotage yourself without even realizing it. For example, if you think you're not worthy of a specific job, you may downplay your professional experience in an interview and not provide enough vivid examples of what you've accomplished.

If you don't fully process your feelings and investigate your beliefs and needs, you run the risk of turning unprocessed feelings into fixed thoughts or limiting beliefs about yourself.

In contrast, an *empowering belief* is a deeply rooted way of thinking about yourself and the world that is optimistic and hopeful. Recognizing and cultivating your empowering beliefs will help you stay connected to your positive emotions and increase your self-confidence. And it will empower you in your job search.

COMMON BELIEFS IN THE JOB SEARCH

LIMITING BELIEFS	EMPOWERING BELIEFS
With the current economy and high unemployment, there are few opportunities.	While there is high unemployment, people are still getting jobs, and I'm confident I will find one too.
I don't think I'll find a job that's as good as my current one, even though I don't like my current job.	I'm fully capable of getting a job that is as good or better than my current one.
Previous jobs ended up being such disappointments. I've lost faith that things are going to work out for me.	I can take charge of my life and create a future that I want. That includes getting a great job, even if it doesn't look exactly the way I imagined.
I have to hide parts of my personality and/or compartmentalize myself to fit in or be successful.	I am committed to embracing as much of my authentic self as possible.
I didn't have what I needed to be successful in my last role, and I don't know that I can be successful in my next job.	I am committed to always growing and learning no matter my circumstances. I'm capable of finding the resources I need to be successful.

What limiting and empowering beliefs do you have?

LIMITING BELIEFS   EMPOWERING BELIEFS

_____   _____

_____   _____

_____   _____

Celebrate **AND MAINTAIN MOMENTUM**

You're off to a great start! We hope you have a good sense of what's motivating you and what feelings, needs, and beliefs are helping you or getting in the way of your search. Now you're ready to learn the Emotional Breakthrough Process, which will help you work with your emotions throughout your search.

Chapter 2

THE EMOTIONAL BREAKTHROUGH PROCESS

Stay in a <u>PRESENT</u> mindset

Break through difficult emotions

Start the Emotional Breakthrough
Process for difficult emotions

Manage your work trauma

Amplify positive emotions

Use the Emotional Breakthrough
Process for positive emotions

Celebrate and maintain momentum

Jonathan NEEDS A BREAK-THROUGH

Jonathan was really excited about a fundraising job in the arts, and he was given an indication that he'd probably get an offer. When he wasn't offered the job, he felt misled, disappointed, and frustrated. He started to blame himself for believing that he was going to get the job and for not being good enough to receive an offer.

Using the Emotional Breakthrough Process, Jonathan connected to his difficult feelings and noticed that they were showing up in his body as tightness in his chest. He acknowledged that he had a right to feel angry and be upset.

Jonathan decided to write a letter to the hiring manager that he knew he would never send as a way to process his feelings. This helped Jonathan feel empowered and a sense of closure and peace. Upon reflecting further, Jonathan decided to be more diligent in the future by asking more probing questions about an organization's culture and hiring process. He also committed to a daily morning practice to uncover his feelings and needs.

The effort to find a job is demanding, both emotionally and physically. We've created the Emotional Breakthrough Process to help you be an "emotional athlete" to manage the ups and downs of the search. Just like athletes who prioritize healthy eating and exercise as they train for a big competition, you too need to build healthy behaviors.

In this chapter, we detail step-by-step ways to process and redirect your emotions using the Emotional Breakthrough Process[3]. The breakthrough process will help you get more connected to the feelings and underlying needs and beliefs you've just explored in chapter 1, and, ultimately, your power. While we depict the breakthrough process in a linear fashion, sometimes the steps can happen simultaneously or in a different order.

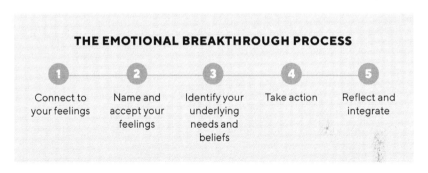

THE EMOTIONAL BREAKTHROUGH PROCESS

1. Connect to your feelings
2. Name and accept your feelings
3. Identify your underlying needs and beliefs
4. Take action
5. Reflect and integrate

As you work through the steps in the Emotional Breakthrough Process, you'll see that your feelings are not facts. They're important signs that point to underlying needs and beliefs you may have.

By engaging with your emotions directly, you'll build a more productive, healthy mindset to become an emotional athlete!

3 Our approach recognizes that your feelings are always valid and it's important to take time to acknowledge them. Annette Stanton et al., "Coping Through Emotional Approach: Scale Construction and Validation," *Journal of Personality and Social Psychology*, 78(6), (2000): 1150–1169, https://doi.org/10.1037/0022-3514.78.6.1150.

When you're just starting out, it can take time to become skilled at the Emotional Breakthrough Process. Be patient with yourself. You may also want to consider additional support such as a career coach or therapist, just like athletes who work with a coach. Once you've had some practice with the breakthrough process, it's likely that you'll be able to move through it in a few minutes or less on your own.

In this chapter, we'll also introduce the concept of *work trauma*—a professional experience that causes you psychological pain or anguish—that may follow you from one job to the next. You'll walk away with practical exercises to deal with emotional hijacks and difficult feelings that you can come back to over and over again, long after you've landed a great job!

Stay in a **PRESENT** Mindset

We introduced the present mindset in the last chapter, and in this chapter we encourage you to continue building it because it's so important to your search. A present mindset is one of the best ways you can access the Emotional Breakthrough Process. Pay attention to how you feel in your body and what thoughts are running through your head as you read this. In chapter 3, we'll share additional ways to set up daily structures to help you be more present.

One immediate way to get into a present mindset is to spend 5-10 minutes journaling about your "monkey brain"—all those simultaneous thoughts that speed through most people's heads every day. As you document the thoughts you have, do your best to notice them without judgment. If you find yourself judging your thoughts, notice that too.

Set a timer for 5 minutes and write down any thoughts you have, regardless of whether you believe them or not. Transcribe your thoughts verbatim, i.e., *I'm really into this activity, although I'm not sure if I'm ready to go deep. What am I having for lunch today? Ugh, this is so much work.*

Break Through Difficult Emotions

The human brain is built for emotional hijackings. That is, our limbic system and neural connections are highly sensitized and triggered to overreact in order to protect us. In fact, we evolved these instinctive reactions as a defense mechanism. What used to be a wolf or lion on the savannah in ancient times is now your manager making a snide comment at work about your judgment or a colleague dismissing what you think is a brilliant idea. This may make you feel flushed, with a racing heartbeat, and flooded with emotion. It may make it difficult to stay focused and in the present. When you're emotionally hijacked, you'll likely feel overwhelmed, or alternately, you might shut down and feel numb and disconnected.

We understand that connecting to your difficult feelings might be the last thing you want to do. You don't even want to know how many chocolate bars Lauren and Cathy ate while writing this book! The Emotional Breakthrough Process is designed to make it as easy as possible to work with your feelings and help you cope if you find yourself shutting down, repressing, or denying your feelings.[4]

---

4 Note that in the first few chapters of this book, we use the specific terms that comprise "vulnerabilities," such as difficult emotions, unmet needs, limiting beliefs, and triggers. Later in the book, especially in chapter 4, we use "vulnerabilities" as an umbrella term.

SHORTCUTS TO DEAL WITH AN EMOTIONAL HIJACK

HOW TO REACT	WHAT TO DO	HOW THIS HELPS
1. Pause and stop what you're doing. Give yourself some space to get calm.	Take a break or a nap or meditate. *"I'm going to go for a walk and will come back and see if I can better understand what's underneath my feelings."*	Resisting a hijack is likely to worsen the experience. By creating distance, you'll be more ready to address your emotions directly.
2. Accept the hijack.	Accept that you're in the middle of a hijack by acknowledging it. If you can't, try saying something like: *"I'm not able to accept this feeling at this time."*	Doing so brings you closer to being able to accept what's happening, because you're acknowledging the reality of your feelings and experience.
3. Interrupt your hijack.	You might say, *"I feel panicked. My feelings are a message that I need to pay attention to my reaction."*	Narrating what's happening to you in the moment creates space to get perspective and will help calm your nervous system down.

If you ignore or deny your feelings, they won't go away, but rather they will fester and operate "underground" outside your consciousness, creating obstacles to your search.

Review the chart and start to think about what difficult emotions you might be experiencing as you prepare to use the Emotional Breakthrough Process.

HOW DIFFICULT EMOTIONS TRICKLE
INTO THE JOB SEARCH

SAD	You may mourn the loss of a particular identity or status. Or you might miss working with colleagues and clients you like.
DISCOURAGED OR FRUSTRATED	When you don't hear back after submitting an application or having an interview, you may feel discouraged or frustrated, especially if this happens repeatedly.
ANXIOUS	It's natural to worry about what the future holds, especially if you were fired or ended a job on a challenging note. It can be scary to figure out how to make ends meet and not find a job soon enough to avoid debt.
BORED	The job search requires a tremendous amount of focus without necessarily providing much entertainment! It's easy to get distracted.
OVERWHELMED OR EXHAUSTED	It may feel like your "to do" list is never-ending. If you're working while looking for a new job, you may feel perpetually tired.
ASHAMED OR EMBARRASSED	At different points in your search, you may feel like there's something wrong with you if you don't make obvious progress like getting an interview. You may feel inadequate, bringing up feelings of shame.
ANGRY	Because it can seem like there's so much out of your control, you might feel powerless, which can cause anger. This feeling is intensified when you dislike your current job or are confused about what to do next.
ISOLATED OR LONELY	The job search can feel lonely and isolating, especially when you're not feeling fully supported by friends and family. The isolation of pandemic life has exacerbated this feeling for many people. Moreover, sometimes it can feel like everyone around you is successful except for you.
SELF-DOUBTING OR CONFUSED	Confusion and self-doubt are likely to emerge throughout your search, especially if you're unsure of what you want to do next or where to begin. This feeling is amplified if you've been fired or had a challenging work situation in the past.

Start the Emotional Breakthrough Process for *Difficult Emotions*

1. Connect to your feelings

The most critical first step is acknowledging your difficult feelings. Start by taking a few breaths to slow down and notice what sensations you're experiencing. Connect with your body and get out of your head.

Pay attention to what you're feeling, not what you're thinking about what you're feeling. Facing a high-stakes job interview, you might, for example, feel constriction inside your stomach or a tightening of your chest. These physical sensations are clues that you're experiencing an important emotion. Another sign that you're in the throes of a difficult emotion is that your mind might be racing with thoughts, likely connected to the physical sensations you're feeling.

2. Name and accept your feelings

Once you're connected to your emotions, it's important to name them, using the list of common emotions on page 21 as a starting point.[5] Multiple emotions almost always show up at once, forming an emotional knot. So, when you're trying to identify what you're truly feeling, it's important to identify each thread. If you don't, it's difficult to access the wisdom within each distinct feeling and create enough distance from your emotions to name them.

Next, turn your attention to accepting that you feel the way you do even if you wish you didn't! When you accept your feelings, you're

---

5 "Affect labeling," or putting feelings into words, helps diminish strong emotional reactions. A 2007 study using an MRI showed that affect labeling decreased the amygdala response to negative emotions and other limbic areas. Lieberman et al., "Putting Feelings into Words: Affect Labeling Disrupts Amygdala Activity in Response to Affective Stimuli," *Psychological Science*, (May 2007): 421-428, https://doi.org/10.1111/j.1467-9280.2007.01916.x.

implicitly recognizing what's happening in the moment and are more available to understand what's at the root of your feeling. It's totally normal to not want to feel sad or anxious, for instance, but resisting your emotions will only make them grow.

Take a few moments to name any negative emotions you're feeling right now as you think about your job search.

_____

_____

_____

Take a few moments to get still. What sensations, if any, are present for you as you think about your job search today?

_____

_____

3. Identify your underlying needs and beliefs

As we've said, feelings are the gateway to your needs and beliefs. When you're able to truly understand what needs and beliefs are at the heart of your feelings, you have more power to change your situation. You can then remove obstacles that prevent you from focusing on job search tasks.

When you're experiencing a difficult emotion, there's often an unmet need or limiting belief underneath. For instance, when you explore your anxiety, you might recognize that you have a need to feel competent and you're worried about what's ahead. Knowing that your need to feel competent is manifesting as anxiety can help you develop strategies to address the real source of anxiety and discover other ways that you might be able to meet your need (competence).

Pick 1–2 emotions and reflect on what unmet needs and/or limiting beliefs you have. It helps to start a sentence with *"I need..."* or *"A belief I have about myself is..."*

4. Take action

After you identify your feelings and underlying needs and beliefs, you can start to shift your attention from reflection to action. If you need validation or recognition and you're not getting that in your job search at the moment, you might decide to pursue volunteer work, a side project, or even unpaid work that keeps you energized. Or you may decide that the best way for you to redirect feelings of anxiety or incompetence is to edit your résumé or finish your cover letter, helping you connect to your self-worth and feel more confident.

ADDITIONAL WAYS TO REDIRECT NEGATIVE EMOTIONS

▶ Write down a short rant about what's bothering you and then burn it.

▶ Vent to a friend or trusted ally.

▶ Adjust your posture, whether you're seated or walking, so you're able to shift your emotions to a more manageable level.

▶ If you're experiencing an emotion that makes you feel really small, try acting as if you're bigger, bolder, and more confident. You might decide to put on an outfit that makes you feel really good about yourself!

▶ Focus on a positive memory to reset your mood. But be wary of simply trying to replace a difficult emotion with a positive one.

What immediate actions, if any, would be most helpful to take, based on your feelings and underlying needs and beliefs?

_____

_____

5. Reflect and integrate

To really develop into an emotional athlete, you'll need to regularly take stock of what you're learning about yourself through the breakthrough process, especially if you're new to working with your emotions. It's easy to move quickly through this step, but do your best to make the time to reflect and integrate what you're learning. You'll likely notice themes and patterns, such as when you tend to feel certain emotions, what your core needs are, and the types of beliefs you have about yourself.

What have you learned about how you process your emotions and how it impacts your day-to-day work on your job search?

_____

_____

One of Cathy's clients, a technology consultant in their thirties, felt shame about criticism they had received from a few of their previous managers. In their coaching work with Cathy, they explored what beliefs and needs they had, and it turns out that one of their needs was to be recognized as competent. They realized that throughout their life they'd been extrinsically motivated. They sought feedback as a way to feel validated instead of owning their own worth. They had been unable to figure out how to move forward in their search because they felt an overwhelming sense of shame and a deep belief around the need to be perfect in order to be okay. With this newfound understanding, they were able to acknowledge their accomplishments and found ways to build their own sense of self-worth. It was a turning point for them. Soon after, their job search accelerated!

Manage Your Work Trauma

It's surprising how many clients we've worked with who have had work trauma but haven't realized it or have spent years denying it. Work trauma can run the gamut—it can be a one-time event or something that consistently happened over time in multiple work settings. These experiences negatively impact your sense of self. For example, one of Cathy's clients had a direct report who was undermining her leadership by gossiping about her to other staff. This behavior caused her to question whether she was capable of building strong relationships, affecting her as she applied to jobs.

If you're part of a group that's historically oppressed, you've likely experienced some form of work trauma, such as not being included in a major team decision or being overlooked for an internal position. This not only affects your self-perception but also makes it more difficult to work with your emotions if they've been denied in the past.

Part of what's so challenging about work trauma is that it can be difficult to realize that you're experiencing it in the moment.

Most people go into a primal reaction as it's happening—fight, flight, or freeze. You might not have heard of a fourth reaction: fawn.

Fawning occurs when we please or placate others as a way to overcompensate for someone else's bad behavior. It might show up after your manager has berated you at a staff meeting about some aspect of your performance, and you overcompensate by working long hours even though you've already been working at your highest capacity.

Our flight, fight, freeze, or fawn responses can be helpful because they momentarily protect us, which is why we have these automatic reactions in the first place. However, if you don't interrupt these patterns using the breakthrough process, you won't be able to shift the situation you find yourself in because your defense mechanisms will mask your underlying needs.

Our clients have reported feeling shame, fear, embarrassment, and other difficult feelings when they're experiencing work trauma. One of Cathy's clients, an easygoing and talented writer, was fired without being given a reason; the lingering sense of not knowing or understanding why he had been let go made him feel dejected. He worried that there was something wrong with him and that he would falter in his next job.

Unpacking work trauma, whether big or small, is very challenging to do alone. It's often helpful to seek professional help to develop strategies to move forward. We encourage you to be mindful about how you share work trauma with family, friends, and colleagues, as many people aren't prepared for this type of conversation, and it may cause more pain for you to expose your vulnerability to them.

Jot down any memories of work trauma that you've experienced that might impact your job search.

SELF-SABOTAGE: THE SECOND ARROW

Be mindful that when you're doing deep work with your feelings, needs, and beliefs, it's common to experience judgment not only about your feelings, but also about your reaction to your feelings. This is described as the second arrow in the Buddhist tradition. **The idea is that if you're hit by an arrow, try not to make it worse by shooting yourself with a second arrow.**

First Arrow:
You have a good interview, but you are upset by how you responded to a specific question.

Second Arrow:
You judge yourself for how you reacted.

You may be wondering why you're overreacting and so sensitive, especially when you felt like you had a good interview overall. You might even make up a story in your head about why you're feeling upset. This can leave you feeling even more upset and/or frustrated.

Creating a story for why something happened may take on a life of its own, making you feel even worse, aka the second arrow! In other words, don't self-blame! Instead, turn to the breakthrough process to discover your underlying needs, using them as a catalyst for action.

Amplify Positive Emotions

Now we're going to shift gears to use the Emotional Breakthrough Process for positive emotions. Sometimes more attention is given to dealing with difficult emotions than positive ones. Knowing when to push the gas pedal on feel-good emotions can help you bring more ease and even joy into your search.[6]

Embracing and amplifying your positive emotions will help you think more positively and creatively and help you to take action in your search. Positive feelings also increase alertness, your ability to see possibilities and problem-solve, and so much more. Plus, feelings are contagious; your positive feelings are likely to breed more feel-good emotions in yourself and others.[7]

Use the Emotional Breakthrough Process for *Positive Emotions*

In the breakthrough process for difficult emotions, you use your feelings to identify unmet needs, whereas with feel-good emotions, you identify met needs. In both cases, you're learning to unwrap the needs and beliefs inside your feelings so you can discern what actions to take in your search.

1. Connect to your feelings

It can be difficult to recognize what positive emotions feel like. In our experience, the physical sensations include an overall sense of lightness and more energy. We recommend sitting with and marinating in your positive emotions *when you're experiencing*

---

6 Amplifying positive emotions in the moment and over the longer term supports overall well-being and psychological growth. This also has been referred to as "upward spiral theory of lifestyle change." Barbara Fredrickson, "The Role of Positive Emotions in Positive Psychology," *American Psychologist*, (March 2001): 218-216, https://doi.org/10.1037/0003-066X.56.3.218. Barbara Fredrickson and Thomas Joiner, "Reflections on Positive Emotions and Upward Spirals." *Perspectives on Psychological Science* 13(2), (March 2018):194-199. https://doi.org/10.1177/1745691617692106.

7 While emotional contagion is well documented, newer data suggests that emotions may even be transferred via social networks, outside of in-person interactions. Adam Kramer, Jamie Guillory and Jeffrey Hancock, "Experimental Evidence of Massive-Scale Emotional Contagion Through Social Networks," *PNAS*, 111(24), (June 2014): 8788-8790, https://doi.org/10.1073/pnas.1320040111.

them, allowing those good vibes to circulate in your system. Remember that the physical sensations inside your body will help you identify how you're feeling. If you're having trouble noticing what your positive emotions are, try paying attention to the absence of negative feelings or thoughts.

Take a few moments to get still and notice what sensations, if any, are present for you, as you think about your desire to get a great job.

---

2. Name and accept your feelings

Connect with your feel-good emotions, using the list on page 21 in chapter 1 as a guide. When you name the positive feeling you're having, you can help cement the experience that accompanies it. For example, if you finish a first draft of your résumé and you're feeling a sense of pride or happiness, cultivate that feeling by writing down or saying to yourself, *"I finished the first draft of my résumé. It wasn't easy to get started, but I pushed through and did it!"*

Name the positive emotions you're feeling right now.

---

3. Identify your underlying needs and beliefs

Next, identify which of your needs are being met and what empowering beliefs are influencing you. For example, if you complete a cover letter and you get a call back, you might feel excited and eager to have a conversation. Ask yourself: What specifically is making me so happy about hearing back? Perhaps you have a met need connected to recognition and being valued. Or maybe hearing back reinforces your belief that you can and will get a job that you really want.

As you explore your feel-good emotions, take some time to reflect or write about what underlying needs have been met and what specific beliefs or thoughts helped you to meet them.

Pick a positive emotion and ask yourself: What need is being met? What empowering belief do I have about myself that allows me to experience this emotion?

---

4. Take action

As we mentioned previously, the breakthrough process isn't linear—indeed, you're taking action consistently as you connect to your feel-good emotions and explore what's under the surface.

One way to amplify positive emotions is to bring up a memory and observe the visual details in it. The amazing thing is that your brain interprets that memory as if it's happening to you now—that's a lot of good mojo to get you energized in your search! Try picturing all of your friends at a party showering you with love or a vista that makes you happy. If you're not a visual person, you might choose to write a sentence that summarizes the memory that you can revisit. *"I felt so supported when I talked to my three friends last week."*

Another way to take action is to find something outside your job search that connects you to positive emotions, whether it's a child in your life, nature, or something else you find inspiring. For example, while Lauren was interviewing for a new job, she took daily walks with her toddler. Getting outside and focusing on her little one made her feel more alive and increased the feel-good emotions she needed to help her stay grounded and present in her job search.

What, if any, immediate actions could you take to maximize the positive emotions that you experience in your job search?

_____

_____

_____

5. Reflect and integrate

As you get more connected to your feel-good emotions, notice which of your needs are met and what feelings and beliefs are most present for you. Think about how you want to maximize your feel-good emotions and how they help you stay in a healthy and productive mindset during your job search.

What have you learned about the helpful role that positive emotions can play in your job search? Jot down any additional observations you have about your met needs and empowering beliefs.

_____

_____

_____

TRANSFORM THE VOICES IN YOUR HEAD
TO HEALTHY SELF-TALK

We all have thousands of thoughts every day that influence us, both consciously and unconsciously. Bringing consciousness to how you narrate your experience will give you many data points on what's motivating you and what's holding you back. As you engage more deeply in understanding how your thoughts are influencing you, you'll have a much greater ability to transform them into healthy self-talk.

MAXIMIZE POSITIVE EMOTIONS IN YOUR JOB SEARCH

JOYFUL/HAPPY	Schedule "happy breaks" throughout the day. Do something uplifting such as listening to music, having a dance party, or reading a good book.
HOPEFUL/ OPTIMISTIC	Make a bucket list of all the things that you're looking forward to and/or want to do in the next 1–5 years.
INSPIRED	Create and keep a list of people, ideas, places, art, etc., that energize and inspire you. We call this your Inspiration and Advisory Board (more details in chapter 5).
PEACEFUL	Consider turning off your technology or going out into nature. Declutter your physical space.
CURIOUS	Follow your curiosities. Attend a webinar or talk with a friend or colleague about a topic that you're interested in.
DETERMINED	Take a few moments to recall a memory where you gave it your all and bask in gratitude.
PROUD	Think back to your proudest personal or professional achievement. Spend a moment or two really reflecting on that memory and how you felt when it happened.
CELEBRATORY	Do something nice for yourself, like treating yourself to a delicious meal.
ENERGIZED/EXCITED	Picture yourself on the first day of your new job. You're about to start important and fulfilling work. See if you can bring some of that excitement into your search!
CONFIDENT/CERTAIN	Ask a friend to share what they admire or respect about you.

Celebrate
AND MAINTAIN MOMENTUM

Take a moment to give yourself props for reading this book—not everyone is willing to do this type of work—so kudos to you! By working with difficult and feel-good emotions, you'll be able to become more of an emotional athlete, accessing the full range of your feelings and directing them in a way that helps you build your self-confidence, self-awareness, and power. We strongly encourage you to continue on this journey of working with the Emotional Breakthrough Process as you move through your search and beyond.

Chapter 3

SET UP YOUR SEARCH FOR SUCCESS

Get into a <u>PRACTICAL</u> mindset

Establish daily practices

Determine your optimal work-rest cycle

Set up your schedule

Break your tasks into bite-size pieces

Track your progress

Create your support team

Be open to changing direction

Celebrate and maintain momentum

Diego GETS ORGANIZED

Forty-three-year-old Diego is a classic ideas guy, a fan of having deep conversations with colleagues and mentoring others. Last year, he came to Cathy for help in finding a new job. He had a successful career as a finance executive, but he was struggling to land a new position.

When Cathy met with him, she found him brimming with thoughts, yet deeply overwhelmed. He had recently become a new dad and felt pressure to find a job that worked for him. Cathy noticed that while he really needed help with tactics, Diego was prioritizing community building. He was spending several hours each week meeting with professional contacts—but he hadn't updated his LinkedIn profile. He didn't have an intentional approach to structuring his time, including details such as where and how he was actively working on his job search.

Through coaching, Diego soon realized that his childcare responsibilities were distracting him more than he realized. He decided to negotiate time with his partner to balance being a caregiver and made a small space in their bedroom for a desk where he could work. To make the volume of activities—brainstorming jobs, writing his résumé, analyzing job postings, etc.—more manageable, Cathy helped him break them into bite-size tasks. Getting organized made Diego feel much more grounded and lowered his anxiety. It also helped him to know exactly what to do and when.

In chapters 1 and 2, you increased your awareness of your feelings and how to work with your underlying needs and beliefs using the Emotional Breakthrough Process. Now, it's time to switch gears and set up the tactical aspects of your search so you can stay organized.

Just as we coached you to become an emotional athlete in chapter 2, now we're going to support you in further developing your "training regimen." We'll introduce you to the concepts of optimal work-rest cycle and bite-sizing your job search, so you can best allocate your energy, focus, and time. You'll start to develop healthy habits for tracking your progress and creating support structures that will serve you in the long term.

Getting a good job takes time; there is no getting around it. The average job search for our clients typically takes between three to twelve months—averaging six months.

We've found that it usually takes about 1–3 hours a day, or 5–15 hours per week to get a great job. This number often surprises our clients, as they tend to think they should be working full-time on their search.

Spending less time on your search might not lead you to the results you're hoping for and could prolong the process. But spending more time means you risk burnout. Your weekly commitment will likely wax and wane depending on your energy and where you are in the process, with more time up front. You'll need to experiment with what works best for you. Over time, you'll discover what you need to increase your productivity and flow, which will also help you to excel in your new job.

Get into a **PRACTICAL** Mindset

As you move from the breakthrough process into the more tactical aspects of your search, you'll need to switch mindsets. There's no doubt that getting present will help you be more available to focus on the tasks ahead. Additionally, getting practical will make the day-to-day work of your job search more doable.

Start by asking yourself when you ideally want to begin a new role. Think about the demands of your current job (if you have one), family commitments, health concerns and big changes coming up like family moves. How available, realistically, can you be for your job search on a daily basis? It's nearly impossible to apply for jobs or interview when you're tired or feeling out of sorts. You need a healthy body and mind, so ensure that your most basic needs are met by making a commitment to your own health.

Some of the commitments our clients have made as they begin their search include:

- Prioritizing a healthy diet
- Getting regular exercise
- Creating good sleep habits
- Avoiding work related to the job search on the weekend, if possible
- Setting up a dedicated workspace

Take a moment to jot down any commitments that you would like to make in your search.

_____

_____

_____

Establish Daily Practices

We can't emphasize enough the importance of having a regular practice to get centered and focused. It will be a game changer in your job search and in your life!

Daily practices provide a structure and space to nurture the mindsets we describe in the book. They also offer a way to slow down and live and work more intentionally, resisting our current workaholic culture.

You might be thinking, *"I have a million things to do to finish my résumé and apply to jobs. I don't have time to do a daily practice."* We so get it and have been there ourselves! Yet even 2–5 minutes a day can help you start to shift into a new mindset, build your confidence, and increase your awareness of what you really want.

Know that as you build your daily practices, resistance will likely creep in. You might find yourself snoozing your alarm when it's time to wake up, or consistently skipping over the time you set aside for your meditation. Recognizing that you have resistance is a good thing! You can start to learn where you might be blocked so you can get unblocked.

Morning Practice

A morning practice gets you into the right mindset to face the job search tasks ahead. Keep it short, simple, and sweet. For Cathy and Lauren, a regular morning practice has made a huge difference in their lives and allowed them to accomplish big goals, including writing this book! Meditation has been a staple in Cathy's life for a long time—she even took a sabbatical to live on an ashram and study meditation in-depth. It's not necessary to live on an ashram or take a sabbatical to develop daily practices (although it does help!).

If you already have a routine that works for you, reflect on what you might want to adjust. Below are some ideas for your morning practice:

Reflect on your feelings and needs

Take a few moments to identify what feelings are present and what action you might take to meet your needs. Are your basic needs met? Are you hungry and/or tired? What job search tasks do you want to work on? Write down a few of the bite-size tasks you want to focus on today.

If you're feeling closed off or unable to connect to your feelings and/or underlying needs and beliefs, reflect on what would help you, whether it's a walk outside or a conversation with a friend. If you find that you have a number of unmet needs, prioritize one or two that you can take some action on, using the Emotional Breakthrough Process.

Express gratitude

Gratitude, as you may already know, is a powerful way to get connected to yourself and others.[8] If you choose to do a self-gratitude practice, turn inward to examine what you're grateful for about yourself. Or you can extend gratitude outward as you identify people, places, or things that fill you with appreciation. You may find it helpful to journal or share a gratitude practice with a friend.

Practice breathwork, mindfulness, and/or meditation

We encourage you to try different meditation classes, books, and apps. Find an approach that works for you. Meditation and mindfulness are timeless and proven methods for building inner wisdom and resilience. Lauren and Cathy are both big fans of breathing exercises and mindful meditation. For instance, Cathy starts her day with ten minutes of meditation focused on breathwork.

Develop a morning mantra or tagline

One way to start your morning practice is to write a mantra or tagline describing how you want to feel as you work on your job search. What energizes and motivates you? It might be a quote from James Baldwin, a poem by Mary Oliver, or something that you write yourself. For years, Lauren listened to a morning mantra that she wrote and recorded on her phone.

LAUREN'S MORNING MANTRA
I start this day
Awake and alert
Ready for anything
Powered by my desire to make
a difference
Guided by my intuition
Inner strength, beauty and wisdom
Love and compassion

I can choose how I spend my time
And how I show up
And how I treat my body
I am mindful of what I put into my body
And how I take care of it

There is so much to learn and so much to do
I am excited for what is possible

Get moving

Many of our clients exercise in the morning, whether it's a run, bike ride, or yoga class. It may sound cliché, but getting out of your head and into your body can be really helpful when you're feeling fatigued by the search process. Even a ten-minute workout can make a difference. Cathy does fifteen minutes of stretches, yoga,

---

8 A gratitude practice has been shown to lead to better physical health and well-being, at home and in the workplace. Armenta, Christina N., Megan M. Fritz, and Sonja Lyubomirsky, "Functions of positive emotions: Gratitude as a motivator of self-improvement and positive change." *Emotion Review 9*, no. 3 (2017): 183-190, https://doi.org/10.1177/1754073916669596.

and Pilates after her morning meditation and finds that it really helps her focus and think more clearly in her day.

Based on the possibilities listed above, what are your initial ideas for a morning practice?

_____

_____

Evening Practice

When you have a good handle on your morning practice, consider adding an evening practice of 2–10 minutes to close out your day on an intentional note. Having an evening routine can help you declutter your mind and let go of the day's activities.

One idea is to create an evening mantra or phrase such as _"I let go of today and am ready for deep rest."_ You may choose to do a gratitude practice or read a poem. Whatever you decide to do in the evening, make sure that it's restful and relaxing; you don't need to take any action—that can wait until tomorrow!

EVENING SELF-GRATITUDE PRACTICE

- Find a place you can sit quietly and comfortably.
- Feel your feet on the floor and your back against a chair or another surface.
- Let your focus drift slowly to your body, from your toes up to your head, and notice any sensations.
- Reflect on at least one action you took to move your search forward, no matter how small.
- Thank yourself for making the time and putting in the effort. If you don't feel like you did enough, briefly reflect on what got in the way and recommit to doing something tomorrow.
- Note anything that you are grateful for and remind yourself that tomorrow is a new day.

What are your initial ideas for a regular evening practice?

Determine Your Optimal Work-Rest Cycle

In a 24/7 work world where workaholism and blurred work-life boundaries are the norm, it's more critical than ever to slow down but more difficult to do so.

As we write this chapter, COVID-19 has increased the pressures of home workloads and childcare, making quiet time even more challenging to find, and, perhaps for that very reason, even more important to carve out.

That's why knowing your optimal work-rest cycle is key—that is, what you need to include in your daily schedule and what you should omit to do your best work and maximize your energy, focus, and creativity.

We think that slowing down and getting in touch with your optimal work-rest cycle is revolutionary and helps to counter our "always on" culture. When you're in touch with your optimal work-rest cycle, you can tune in to your natural rhythms to gauge when you're the most energized and focused throughout the day and when you need rest and relaxation.

OPTIMAL WORK-REST CYCLE	EXAMPLE WORK STYLE
You prefer to take most of your phone calls in the morning to be most engaged.	You have a strong preference for 1:1 conversations that build relationship and connection as opposed to driving towards outcomes.
	You tend to be accommodating in your work, allowing others to take the lead. You've gotten feedback that you should take charge more often.

Your optimal work-rest cycle is highly connected to, but not the same as, what is commonly called work style—how you prefer to get work done and collaborate with others. Knowing your work style will help you clarify what you need to be the most focused and effective.

In order to set up a daily schedule that complements your optimal work-rest cycle and work style, think about what allows you to do your best work when completing both quick tasks and deep work[9]—work that requires more intensive, in-depth attention. And find moments of flow in your day.[10] As you do, you'll likely notice that you're more in sync with yourself and may even feel more motivated.

Think about how you'll organize your weekly schedule to align with your optimal work-rest cycle. You might consider the following:

- Two or three 90-minute "deep work" sessions per week
- A series of 20-30 minute work sessions throughout the day
- 10 minutes of downtime between tasks
- An extended break midday
- Some physical movement
- Daily time for stillness and contemplation
- Scheduling job-related conversations early or later in the day, depending on your energy and attention

Make sure to incorporate enough rest and rejuvenation, especially if you have a job. Check in with yourself to better understand when

---

9 Cal Newport defines deep work as "professional activities performed in a state of distraction-free concentration that push your cognitive capacities to the limit." He was inspired, in part, by Mason Currey's account of Carl Jung's undistracted writing time that he recounted in *Daily Rituals: How Artists Work*. Cal Newport, *Deep Work: rules for focused success in a distracted world* (New York: Grand Central Publishing, 2016).

10 "Flow" is the way people describe their state of mind when consciousness is harmoniously ordered, and they want to pursue whatever they are doing for their own sake. In our ideal world, you'll feel moments of flow in the job search as you take the steps in this book to get a new job. Mihaly Csikszentmihalyi, *Flow: the psychology of optimal experience*. (New York: Harper & Row, 1990).

you feel highly focused and/or motivated and do your best work. You may decide that when things are slow in your search, you need a longer break where you go "job search free" for a few days or even a few weeks to rest and refocus.

What do you need to do your best work? How would you define your optimal work-rest cycle?

_____

_____

_____

_____

A few years ago, a mid-career executive director of an environmental nonprofit in serious need of a new job reached out to Cathy. She had dedicated her life to nonprofit work, yet she was exhausted by a toxic workplace and crushing workload. Board meetings and other events devoured her evenings. And it felt like there was always a fire to put out.

She told Cathy, "I need to leave." Wanting to find a new job quickly was a priority, but Cathy suggested that she take a few weeks off before she started engaging in a full-on job search. She decided to take some time to rest and recharge so when she turned to the job search, she could be more emotionally engaged. She ended up unplugging for three weeks and did a lot of self-talk to rest and heal from what felt like a destructive workplace. Cathy's advice: "Don't think about the job search if possible...really turn it off. And when you start to think about your search, write down any thoughts to revisit later. Redirect your attention to the 'assignment' of resting as much as you can."

Set Up Your Schedule

Before you set up a daily schedule, it's critical to determine if you're really ready to dive into your job search. Like Cathy's client, you might do better to take a break first and then create an energizing daily schedule from a place of renewal.

Most people, even if they don't like rules or rigidity, do better when they have a clear structure to their daily job search activities. Scheduling time and overestimating how much time you'll need for your search, especially if you're also balancing work, will help you follow through. Sometimes we even sit with our clients while they put time on their calendars for specific tasks—it's that important.

SAMPLE DAILY SCHEDULE (ASSUMING ~2 HOURS/DAY)	
2–10 MINUTES PER DAY	Morning practice
20 MINUTES PER DAY	Identify and prioritize bite-size tasks
20 MINUTES PER DAY	Clarify your unique value
20 MINUTES PER DAY	Clarify your ideal work and culture
15 MINUTES PER DAY	Build community and have connected conversations
20–30 MINUTES PER DAY	Create key application materials and prepare for interviews
20–30 MINUTES PER DAY	Manage your personal and job search emails
2–10 MINUTES PER DAY	Evening practice

As you work through the subsequent chapters, you'll have a better sense of the work needed to find a job. Check in with yourself at least once a week—ideally on Friday afternoon or Monday morning—and commit to the tasks you can realistically complete in the upcoming week.

Pause now and map out a rough schedule on your calendar for the next two weeks and, if it's helpful to you, a schedule for the next few months. How aligned is it with your optimal work-rest cycle?

SCHEDULE BUFFER TIME

When you put time on the calendar, be sure to add in buffer time, that is, space that gives you time to rest and rejuvenate as you work. When you have a two-hour deep work session, but we recommend taking at least a ten-minute break, if possible, between tasks. Many of our clients have shared that looking at the news or social media is distracting and draining during these breaks when they want to relax and/or rejuvenate. Instead, grab a cup of tea or spend a few minutes daydreaming. Experiment with what energizes and centers you.

Break Your Tasks into Bite-Size Pieces

Breaking your to do list into bite-size pieces goes a long way to ensure you meet your long-term goals. For example, tackle the first paragraph of your cover letter rather than edit it all at once. You'll want to develop a list of at least 10–20 bite-size tasks that take less than 5–20 minutes to complete, so you can achieve little wins and minimize your feeling of overwhelm.

As you develop your list of bite-size tasks and work on them, start by focusing on what energizes you the most. Consider if it would be more energizing to start something new or continue an existing task that you've been working on. The bite-size tasks add up over time and deliver the dopamine hits that will give you a sense of accomplishment and momentum.

SAMPLE BITE-SIZE TASKS

✔ Work on the summary of expertise for your résumé

✔ Map your community

✔ Research two organizations of interest

✔ Research job titles and functions

✔ Edit the top portion of your LinkedIn profile

✔ Spend 10 minutes focusing on a chart on your unique value

✔ Develop a set of talking points for an upcoming interview

✔ Ask a friend to be an accountability buddy

✔ Update your list of bite-size tasks

Track Your Progress

Consistently review your bite-size tasks and track your progress, whether it's in a paper notebook, an Excel spreadsheet, or an app that helps you stay organized. Cathy still uses an old-school planner, while Lauren likes to use Airtable to organize her job searches. Keeping a progress notebook will help you hold yourself accountable.

PROGRESS NOTEBOOK

DATE	CATEGORY	ACTIVITY	QUESTIONS OR CONCERNS	NEXT STEPS	SUPPORT NEEDED	CELEBRATE!
1/15	Revise my résumé	I worked on the summary of expertise on my résumé.	I feel like what I'm writing sounds generic.	Work for another 20 minutes on my summary of expertise on Wednesday.	Get feedback from my former colleague Samantha tomorrow.	It was hard to get myself to do this today, but I did it!
2/3	Interview prep	I did some research on the organization and wrote a few talking points for an upcoming interview.	I need more practice because I still feel unprepared.	I want to write out a list of questions I might be asked and draft a few talking points.	Ask my partner if he will practice interviewing with me and give me feedback.	I'm proud of taking the time to do this important work—and I think it will pay off!

Create Your Support Team

Your team of family, friends, coworkers, and/or community members is an important sounding board and support squad, cheerleading your search and reminding you why you want a new job, especially when you're feeling down or burned out. In chapter 6, you'll map out your community as part of your outreach. To start building your team now, focus on what immediate support you need.

- **Clarify how you can best engage your support team throughout your search and in what ways.** For example, you might turn to your friend who is a great editor to review your résumé, while you reach out to a former colleague to have a post-interview debrief with you.

- **Find an accountability partner.** If you have a friend or a colleague who is also looking for support in their search, the two of you could regularly check in to stay on track, or schedule mutual work sessions in person or over Zoom.

- **Consider hiring a coach.** You might decide that having someone to work with throughout this time period would help you stay the most committed and motivated (not that we're biased or anything!).

Who do you want on your support team, and how would you

MY TEAM	HOW THEY MIGHT HELP

Be discerning about how you share your job search with your community. Not everyone will agree with how you're approaching your search or get excited about specific jobs that interest you. It's important to stay true to yourself and know when to act on advice and when to say "thanks but no thanks" to feedback (we'll share more on how to do this with what we call the "front door formula" in chapter 6).

Be Open to Changing Direction

If you use a progress notebook or your own version of it, you're more likely to notice if you need to pivot or even make a drastic shift in your search.

Though we don't recommend changing paths just because you had one bad interview or didn't get a job that you were excited about, it's important to recognize when something in your search isn't working or when you have a change of heart about the work you want to do.

At key inflection points in the search, consider the following questions: Are you thinking of shifting directions out of frustration or because you're not seeing immediate results? Or are you looking to change direction after deep reflection on the work you want to do? We encourage you to reach out to your support team to ask for their perspective. At the same time, trust your inner wisdom to guide your decision.

Check in regularly with yourself to gauge if your daily practices and job search schedule are working for you, and make adjustments. You'll know if your morning and evening practices are effective if you notice that you feel more connected to yourself and you automatically do them even without consciously thinking about it. Hopefully you're already noticing that you feel more focused and ready to tackle your job search.

Chapter 4

OWN YOUR UNIQUE VALUE

Get into a GROWTH mindset

Determine your unique value

Map your values

Tap into your skills and experience

Identify your knowledge areas

Document your accomplishments

Clarify your passions and interests

Explore your curiosities

Brainstorm ideas

Embrace your vulnerabilities

Use your unique value

Celebrate and maintain momentum

Simone, a fifty-two-year-old former Peace Corps volunteer, held senior-level operations positions for several top international non-governmental organizations. When she started to look for a new job, she realized that her impressive background wasn't coming across in her résumé and other materials.

The language she was using wasn't inaccurate—she did, in fact, have a "proven track record of success" as her résumé said, and she was, for sure, a "dynamic leader" who had the accomplishments to prove it. In her cover letter, she talked about how she was collaborative, but it felt generic and uninspired. She reached out to Cathy because she wasn't getting the job interviews she expected.

In her work with Cathy, Simone articulated her unique value beyond clichéd résumé-speak. She did the deep work of exploring her skills and diving into her specific accomplishments, for instance, her ability to catalyze collaboration by her authentic ability to relate and connect to others. This started in the Peace Corps, and over time, her ability to create cross-sectoral projects and motivate others was a key to her success.

The exercises she did with Cathy helped Simone articulate her unique value by exploring all the different aspects of herself, including her strengths, ideas, and passions. As a result, she had lots of raw material for her written application materials, and she also felt more assured as she interviewed. Soon enough, she found a great new job at a major NGO.

Tell me about yourself. It's a question you can expect in some form in almost any interview.

You might be inclined to share pithy responses like, *"Ever since college, I've been a social justice activist"* or *"For the last eight years, I've been helping companies with search engine optimization."* But this does not speak to your unique value—the totality of who you are and the unique combination of what you have to contribute to the world.

Why does unique value really matter? It's much more important than helping you answer the "tell me about yourself" question. Understanding yourself better will help you paint a vivid picture of who you are and what you have to offer.

It's not about boasting or demonstrating that you're better than anyone, but rather highlighting the one-of-a-kind combination of qualities that you bring. We think everyone has a unique value that includes not only strengths but also vulnerabilities.

The core of this chapter is a series of exercises to help you further define your unique value based on what we've seen has been particularly helpful with our clients to gain direction and clarity. Doing these exercises also provides important clues about what type of work you're interested in and will give you the raw material for your résumé, cover letters, and interview preparation. If there are other topics or exercises that help you explore your identity and unique value, go for it.

Get into a <u>GROWTH</u> Mindset

When you have a growth mindset, you're more open to continuously learning about and developing yourself. Having a growth mindset allows you to deeply connect to your unique value and to fully realize your potential. It will also help you identify your strengths and deal with your vulnerabilities if you're able to reframe what you're experiencing as a learning opportunity rather than as a disappointment.

We tend to see our identities, both personally and professionally, as relatively fixed, but the reality is that they aren't! When you see your identity as somewhat fluid, you'll be better able to grow and evolve your unique value over time.

Take a few minutes at the end of your morning practice to reflect on what aspects of yourself you are really energized by and where you might want to grow and develop.

Determine Your Unique Value

As you work through the different charts in the pages that follow, we recommend bite-sizing and focusing on one to two charts at a time; it's likely too overwhelming to do the whole chapter at once! Try taking twenty minutes to work through each chart for starters. Focus on what's most energizing for you and feel free to skip a section if it doesn't speak to you or you feel confused. If you get stuck, you may want to pause and return to the Emotional Breakthrough Process.

WHAT MAKES UP YOUR UNIQUE VALUE

Values: The core principles that motivate you and guide your decisions in life and work, often formed in your upbringing and reinforced through lived experience.

Skills and Experience: What you do well and/or what expertise you have.

Accomplishments: Work you've done that has made a difference—big and small—that you're proud of achieving.

Knowledge Areas: The topics and issues that you know a lot about, regardless of whether the information is tied to your work.

Passions and Interests: Areas of enjoyment that you're currently pursuing.

Curiosities: Interest areas you want to learn more about in the future.

Ideas: Dreams, concepts, or plans you want to bring to fruition.

Vulnerabilities: Difficult emotions, triggers, limiting beliefs, and other blocks.

Map Your Values

Values form the bedrock of your worldview. They stem from factors such as your upbringing, lived experience, and cultural norms, consciously and unconsciously guiding your decisions. They provide a powerful North Star for what's important to you and will serve as a guide as you identify your ideal work and evaluate professional opportunities. We distinguish between your *aspirational values* and your *lived values*—that is, what you think your values are versus how you actually live them day-to-day. Being clear on your lived values will help you make decisions throughout the job search.

EXAMPLE VALUE: **Adventure**	
Is this a lived or aspirational value?	**How could you further incorporate this value in your work?**
Lived	My sense of adventure helps me feel more expansive and full of possibility. I'm daydreaming about starting my own business. If I decide not to start something on my own, I want to make sure that I get to travel in my next gig and my workdays aren't too monotonous.

Tap into Your Skills and Experience

Skills include everything from your ability to communicate or community organize to more technical expertise such as writing code or using a customer relationship management (CRM) tool. Identifying your skills is a useful way to figure out what you might want to focus on in your next job. You'll want to be clear on which skills you want to highlight in your résumé and application materials and which ones aren't as important for you in your next role.

EXAMPLE SKILLS:
Community Outreach, Communication, Fundraising

In what specific way(s) have you used this skill? Describe what you did and what the outcome was.	Based on your experience, how would you summarize your skill set?	Rate your level of energy for this skill on a scale of 1–10 with 10 being the most energized. How does your rating inform your job search?
I developed an art exhibit and fundraiser to raise $5,000 for a youth development program in Ghana.	I'm really good at putting on curated events that bring people from different cultures together. And I'm able to ask people for small and big donations when I believe in an organization's mission.	I'm an 8. I really want to continue to be involved in international youth development programs.

Identify Your Knowledge Areas

Think about the topics you often read about or bring up in conversation at work or at home. Perhaps you read a lot of trade journals and participate in a professional association. Or you have a personal interest in topics like women's health or politics. We encourage you to reflect on what you know a lot about, even if you don't consider yourself an expert. Identifying what you know a lot about may give you ideas about new industries or sectors you might want to explore.

EXAMPLE KNOWLEDGE AREA:
Women's Health

Describe your knowledge area and provide an example of the impact you've had using it.	Rate your level of energy for this knowledge area on a scale of 1–10 with 10 being the most energized. How does your rating inform your job search?
I trained to be a doula, and I read and write often about postpartum depression. Last month, I delivered my first baby!	I'm a 9. I'm really excited about continuing to be a doula as a side passion. In the meantime, I want to look for a full-time job where I can focus on women's health, and in particular, help mothers access useful resources to help cope with the realities of motherhood.

Document Your Accomplishments

Accomplishments come in all sizes. Maybe you created a process that helps streamline a workflow or you patented a software invention. Naming what you've achieved helps you access your power and increase your self-confidence. And, of course, effectively explaining your professional achievements will serve you well in your search. You can adapt what you write below for your cover letter and résumé.

Some of our clients tend to minimize their impact at work by downplaying their accomplishments in their materials or interviews. Know that recognizing your accomplishments can be particularly difficult if you've been overlooked or marginalized in previous jobs. As you work on the chart, be mindful that it may stir up difficult emotions and limiting beliefs. You might find that taking a few moments to do the Emotional Breakthrough Process will help you as you grapple with your feelings about what you've accomplished.

EXAMPLE ACCOMPLISHMENT:
Writing a Play

Describe your accomplishment and how it made a difference.	Rate your level of energy for this accomplishment on a scale of 1–10 with 10 being the most energized. How does your rating inform your job search?
I wrote a play about a dysfunctional family growing up in the Bronx that was produced at a local theatre. Nearly 300 people attended. I think people felt inspired by the production.	I'm a 10. I am going to highlight this accomplishment in a cover letter I'm writing for a position at an arts organization. And I also wonder if I could pursue screenwriting as a freelancer.

Clarify Your Passions and Interests

We encourage you to explore interests that make you come alive and nourish your mind, body, and spirit. This will be particularly helpful as a way to stay energized throughout the job search and help you clarify what you would like to do next. Hopefully you will find a job that allows you to explore your passions and interests in some way. Regardless, passions and interests will provide ongoing sustenance to you in your life.

EXAMPLE PASSIONS AND INTERESTS:
Conservation

Describe your passion/interest.	Rate your level of energy for this passion/interest on a scale of 1–10 with 10 being the most energized. How does your rating inform your job search?
I've enjoyed volunteering in Brazil, where I've done woofing (worldwide opportunities on organic farms) and worked with a small nonprofit focused on deforestation.	10. I've started looking for a position that would allow me to spend time focused on conservation and ideally protecting local ecosystems.

Explore Your Curiosities

Your curiosities are a particularly good way to get more energy for what you might want to do, for example, taking an online course to build negotiation skills or learning to cook. Sometimes, it can be difficult to access your curiosities, especially if you're feeling down or depressed in your search. If that's the case, use the Emotional Breakthrough Process and focus on amplifying your positive feelings to increase your openness to new possibilities.

EXAMPLE CURIOSITY:
Coding

Describe your curiosity.	Rate your level of energy for this curiosity on a scale of 1–10 with 10 being the most energized. How does your rating inform your job search?
I've always enjoyed figuring things out, and a friend suggested I try coding. I'm hooked on online tutorials and optimistic about how this new skill might help me in the job market.	8. I'm going to look into taking a course that would give me access to internships with a tech company, where I can practice what I'm learning.

Brainstorm Your Ideas

Whether you want to start a neighborhood association or create a community of practice inside your company, seeing your ideas exist in the world is motivating and inspiring. Exploring your ideas can help you imagine what's possible and generate new ways of thinking, which can be particularly helpful if you're feeling stuck in your job search. An idea you have may even become the basis for a new position or project you dream up. If you don't have any ideas percolating right now, no worries, they'll emerge in due time.

EXAMPLE IDEA:
Online Makers Lab

Describe your idea.	Rate your level of energy for this idea on a scale of 1–10 with 10 being the most energized. How does your rating inform your job search?
I want to take the traditional model of the in-person maker space and figure out how to bring it online to tackle local and global problems.	10. It's all I can think about. I'm planning to apply for some funding to test, iterate, and execute this idea.

_____

_____

_____

_____

_____

Embrace Your Vulnerabilities

You explored your difficult emotions, triggers, unmet needs, limiting beliefs, and other blocks in chapters 1 and 2. Most people tend to hide their vulnerabilities when they're looking for a job, but they can be an asset when you know how to work with them. For example, if you are often sad, you may better understand other peoples' experience of sadness, increasing your empathy and ability to connect with others. We're not suggesting that you talk about your sadness directly with a potential manager or professional contacts. Rather, you will want to focus on the deep empathy that you bring to your work.

When you're in a growth mindset, you're always looking at ways to use your vulnerabilities to learn and develop. For instance, if you've discovered that you're someone who delays sharing completed work out of fear that it's not good enough, in an interview you might say, "I always check in with colleagues to get feedback at key moments in a project to make sure I'm on track."

It's a courageous act just to face your vulnerabilities! Sharing them takes even more courage and thoughtfulness. As you explore your vulnerabilities, carefully consider what you feel comfortable communicating that will help other people understand your unique value. Always be mindful of what feels appropriate given the context of your work and your relationships.

EXAMPLE VULNERABILITY:
I'm concerned about not making enough money.
(Unmet need)

On a scale of 1–10, to what degree is this vulnerability influencing your job search? Describe how it's impacting you.	What actions can you take to empower yourself in your job search?
I'm a 10. I haven't saved any money since I graduated from college, and I'm now 35. I have a lot of discomfort talking about money, and shame about how little I earn and have saved. Additionally, despite performing well in my jobs, I haven't had high-paying positions, so I'm interested in sectors and organizations that pay well.	I need to figure out exactly how much money I need to earn to feel empowered. I'm going to make an appointment with a financial advisor to further clarify my financial needs.

EXAMPLE VULNERABILITY:
I'm worried that my age is limiting job opportunities and career advancement. (Belief)

On a scale of 1–10, to what degree is this vulnerability influencing your job search? Describe how it's impacting you.	What actions can you take to empower yourself in your job search?
I'm a 9. I worry that I have too much experience and also that others might perceive that I'm overqualified. In my most recent job, I often felt like work was given to younger colleagues because they were seen as more savvy with social media. Sometimes I was teased about being out of touch with the times.	I've done the Emotional Breakthrough Process, and I'm going to accept that I have the right to feel this emotion and validate that I can't change the dominant cultural narrative on my own. I'm committed to showing my fluency with social media without downplaying the amount of experience I have. I feel clear that my current work environment doesn't embrace people of all ages, and I want to find a new job where age diversity is valued.

EXAMPLE VULNERABILITY:
I am so tired of working with people who "talk the talk"
but don't "walk the walk." (Difficult emotion: Frustration)

On a scale of 1–10, to what degree is this vulnerability influencing your job search? Describe how it's impacting you.	What actions can you take to empower yourself in your job search?
I'm a 10. It's extremely frustrating when my manager makes verbal commitments to clients but lets important work fall through the cracks. I want to feel inspired in my job and work with colleagues who have integrity and align their words with their actions.	I believe my concern is valid, and I'm going to allow myself to feel this frustration. I think I can make this situation work for now and try to tactfully give some feedback to my manager. But I may be unable to stay in my job long term. I need to be working in an organization where people are conscious of the alignment between what they say and how they behave—it's one of my deal breakers.

Use Your Unique Value

You've unsurfaced a lot of information about various aspects of who you are. The next step is to identify the major themes you've uncovered and reflect on how you'll use all this raw material for your applications and community building. You'll do much more work on translating your unique value into talking points in chapter 6.

As Lauren did these exercises and looked across common themes of her unique value, she realized how much she likes to bring people together around a shared goal. For her, this meant finding a job where she could work collaboratively inside an organization to drive big ideas forward. Knowing this helped her get really clear about where to spend her time and energy. For Cathy, part of how she arrived at writing this book was further reflecting on her unique value and identifying how important the value of generosity is to her and her strong desire to share what she's learned at this point in her career.

Take some time to go through the charts in this chapter and identify 5–10 aspects of your unique value that you most want to focus on in your next job.

Aspects of your unique value you want to share:
Example: I'm really good at putting on curated events that bring people from different cultures together.

1. _____
2. _____
3. _____
4. _____
5. _____
6. _____
7. _____

8. ....

9. ....

10. _____

Celebrate
AND
MAINTAIN
MOMENTUM

Whew, that was a lot of work! Take time to celebrate what you've discovered. Now that you've articulated your unique value, you'll be much more prepared to share who you *really* are as you have connected conversations and turn to clarifying your ideal work. Throughout your search, these charts can serve as a treasure trove for you, and you can refer to them again and again.

Chapter 5

DETERMINE THE WORK YOU WANT

Get into an <u>IMAGINATIVE</u> mindset

Brainstorm what you want to do

Identify where you want to work

Define your ideal team and colleagues

Know what you need in a manager

Identify what you want to learn

Determine your target salary and benefits

Decide to freelance or work part-time

Test out your ideal work

Define your must-haves and deal breakers

Celebrate and maintain momentum

Lauren (the co-author!) is one of many people who started a new job in the middle of COVID-19. A few weeks into the pandemic, the head of her company assured employees that there wouldn't be any immediate layoffs despite the brewing economic crisis. But in a month's time, her manager told her that she was being furloughed, joining millions of Americans who had lost their jobs.

Disappointed and scared, Lauren took some time to regroup, processing what happened with close friends and family. She knew that she had spent the past six months clarifying what work she truly wanted to do. She had reflected on the aspects of her job that energized her while getting clear on what she desired in her next job, including job titles and the sectors she was interested in.

Lauren was surprised to learn that despite the economic downturn, there were a number of job openings in her area of leadership development and learning. As she reviewed job descriptions, she considered her list of five deal breakers before deciding to apply. Lauren passed on applying for a number of jobs that were appealing but didn't quite energize her or fit her criteria. She also looked to specific companies she was following to see if they had any openings—which is how she came across a role at a tech company focused on learning and upskilling that immediately spoke to her.

It's really tempting to apply for a position immediately after it comes to your attention. We know, we've been there! The fact that there's so much outside your control—such as which companies are hiring and what roles are in high demand—makes taking action a way to temporarily ease your anxiety. However, we strongly urge you to identify what you *really* want in your next job *before* you begin applying.

If you don't take the time up front to define your ideal work from a place of empowerment, you risk allowing others to define it for you.

That doesn't mean you need to take many months in this exploration phase. However, we do recommend taking at least a couple of weeks, if possible, to clarify what you're looking for.

In this chapter, you'll identify your preferences from day-to-day job responsibilities to the kind of manager and organizational culture you seek. If money is tight, we can imagine you saying, *"I need a job, any job, so I can get out of this hole,"* or *"I can aim for the perfect role later."* As a result, you may feel that you need to start applying for jobs right away and can't take the time to work through the exercises in this chapter. Indeed, it might feel like a luxury you can't afford. Keep using the breakthrough process if you get stuck or need a jolt of positivity. If you feel compelled to apply to jobs, go for it, but get clear on what your ideal work is at the same time.

By stepping back and reflecting on what you really want in your work, you're more likely to find a job that you're excited about and one that pays the bills. This will increase the chances of staying in your job, building your skills and community, and having a healthy, positive work life that leads to higher job satisfaction and perhaps a better salary and more opportunities in the future.

Get into an __IMAGINATIVE__ Mindset

As you engage in your morning and evening practices, allow yourself to imagine various possibilities for your ideal work. We know it can be difficult to do this. But even if you can allow yourself five minutes to get into an imaginative mindset, you'll start to open up possibilities for what you really want.

One way to access this mindset is by doing *automatic writing*, also known as stream of consciousness writing. You'll want to set a timer for 30, 60, or 90 second bursts and write continuously, ideally with pen and paper, without placing any limitations on what's possible. This style of writing will help you bypass your rational mind and get down to the core of what you really want.[11]

Respond to the following prompts or come up with your own. As you start automatic writing, imagine where you are, what you're doing, and how you're feeling.

"I feel most fulfilled in my job when I'm doing…"
"The type of manager that is most supportive and helps me grow is…"
"The organizational culture that best matches my values is…"

Brainstorm What You Want to Do

Your dream job may be clear to you right now. You may have even already identified job titles such as "Data Scientist," "Director of Operations," or "Managing Editor." But if you're not yet clear on the ideal role you want, think about what work you would like to focus

---

11   This approach is similar to the Pennebaker paradigm, where continuous, expressive writing to process emotional experiences has been linked to overall improvements in health. We really like Natalie Goldberg's approach and writing exercises in *Writing Down the Bones*. James Pennebaker and Cindy Chung, "Expressive writing: Connections to physical and mental health," The Oxford Handbook of Health Psychology (Oxford, Oxford University Press, 2011): 417–437.

on each day, including the percentage of time you allocate to specific activities.

For instance, you might really enjoy writing grant proposals, but you also like developing strategic partnerships and envisioning new technology solutions. These activities might not seem connected. At this stage, brainstorm *without* constraints to help you think creatively and imagine what's possible rather than coming up with a list of responsibilities for a specific job such as a fundraiser or an IT specialist.

Looking at job postings can spark ideas about what you do and don't want to do. Job titles also may give you a sense of new trends in the field and how different roles in an industry are evolving. As you look at job descriptions, take note of the responsibilities that resonate with you and reflect on what specifically draws you in. Watch out for tasks that make you cringe.

Knowing what you don't want to do is as important as knowing what you want to do!

Think through what tasks and activities energize you that you would welcome as part of your workday. Remember not to limit yourself by what you think a job title should entail or what tasks might feel logically connected.

Tasks You Want to Do	Percentage of Time You Want to Spend on This in a Given Week
Example: Develop an outreach list of prospective donors and/or sales prospects	Example: 10% and 20% during peak fundraising/sales cycles

Tasks You Don't Want to Do

What themes do you notice after reviewing the tasks you want to do and don't want to do?

_____

_____

_____

Identify Where You Want to Work

As you think about what you need to thrive within an organization, consider the following:

- Mission
- Sector/Industry
- Culture
- Structure and decision-making
- Size
- Location

Mission

What organizations do you think are doing the most interesting and important work right now? Do you want to work for an organization with a particular mission such as improving healthcare, providing access to education, or addressing climate change? With the economy and job market increasingly unpredictable, we encourage you to learn about the funding structures to understand the implications for your own job stability.

Start by researching companies/organizations to learn more about their work and how they treat their employees. Look at their websites, their LinkedIn page or social media presence, and their Glassdoor reviews. Talk to folks you know who know them. As you learn about organizations, don't worry about whether they're hiring or not at this point, as there will be plenty of time for that. Rather, focus on what aspects of the organization resonate with you or not.

IDEAL ORGANIZATIONS

Name of organization	What specifically is drawing you to this organization?	How excited are you about this organization on a scale of 1–10, with 10 being the most excited?

Sector/Industry

As you think about where you may want to work and uncover trends about the type of organizations that are appealing to you, you might discover that your preferences are more or less consistent, or they are all over the place. Perhaps the organizations you're most interested in are all in the same industry (e.g., financial services, consumer goods, or health and life sciences) or are focused on a particular product or service (e.g., management consulting, career coaching). You may want to group the organizations you're interested in by sector or industry.

If you're switching sectors or pursuing a job in a new industry, you'll want to focus on your *transferable skills*—that is, skills and experiences that you have that are relevant in multiple contexts. When you're accustomed to working in the nonprofit sector, for example, it might seem daunting to make the case that the skills you have translate at a startup or corporation. But it's common for people to move between sectors, and some employers will view your experience as a strength, not a limitation!

Do additional research on industrywide trends by looking up relevant articles, journals, and/or associations. You'll also want to talk to people who have made similar career moves or work in the sector or industry of interest to you (more on this in the next chapter!). Translate your skills using industry-specific terms— for instance, if you're moving from a fundraising position in the nonprofit sector to a business development role at a company, talk about the underlying skills such as building relationships.

What sectors and/or industries are you interested in learning more about?

_____

_____

_____

Culture

We define organizational culture as the core values and beliefs, cultural practices, and explicit and implicit ways of working. The more aligned you are with an organization's culture, the more you'll feel like you fit in and can fully share your unique value. For example, at Lauren's company, the CEO holds a quarterly culture call with new hires to share the startup's history and answer questions, reflecting a commitment to the organization's mission and culture.

Particular areas to pay attention to regarding culture are:

- What is the structure and content of regular staff meetings?
- How do employees communicate (Slack or email)?
- What processes and technology support everyday work?
- What's the investment in employees' learning and development?
- How much attention is given to employees' well-being?
- What was the organization's response to COVID?
- Is there a focus on antiracism or gender equality, for example? And are there any specific policies and practices in place?

How would you describe your ideal work culture? What organizational practices are most important to you?

Structure and Decision-Making

Understanding how decisions get made inside organizations is important to gauge whether an organization's culture and values align with your own values and needs. The way that organizations approach decision-making is often directly tied to whether they have a hierarchical structure or are more decentralized.

For example, you may have a preference for more open decision-making—that is, understanding how and why decisions are made, although that's not often the norm! Additionally, think about what structures you would like to have in place to collaborate with other teams or departments.

What type of organizational structures best support you? What is your preference for organizational decision-making?

_____

_____

_____

Size

It's helpful to consider the size of an organization and where you might feel the most comfortable working. A small organization may give you autonomy and leeway to experiment with new ideas, for instance, but it might offer fewer professional development opportunities. A larger organization may provide more stability and structure, but it might also have more bureaucracy you have to navigate. Another consideration is when the organization was founded and what its growth trajectory is. It's often easier to recognize what size organization works best for you after you've had varied experience with different sized organizations.

When Lauren was in her job search, she knew that the roles she was considering worked best with companies that had 300 – 1,500 employees. She had previously worked for a family foundation with 100 employees and at a management consulting firm with close to 400,000 people. Zeroing in on the size and stage of the startup helped Lauren get clear immediately on whether positions were a good fit for her.

Based on what you know about how you like to work and your unique value, what size organizations do you want to consider?

_____

_____

_____

Location

There is much more possibility in a post-COVID world to live in a different location from where you work. It is still a consideration though, especially if there's an expectation that you need to be in person and/or in a physical office. Commute time is often an important factor in deciding where you want to work. Lauren is grateful that her job is completely virtual, although there are a number of global offices if she decides that she wants to relocate. This flexibility was very appealing to her!

Where would you ideally like to live and work?

What locations would you consider for the right job?

_____   _____

_____   _____

_____   _____

Define Your Ideal Team and Colleagues

You'll be happier and more productive when you're able to connect authentically with your colleagues. Finding a team where you are appreciated can be transformational, allowing you the space to share your unique value and contribute in meaningful ways. If there is a lack of alignment, you may feel uninspired or discouraged.

Take a moment to reflect on the following questions:
- What has allowed you to build trust and connection with colleagues in the past? And what has gotten in the way?
- Exactly how do you like to collaborate with your team?
- What work style and personality in a teammate do you know definitely does and doesn't work for you?
- How often would you like to meet with your team—daily or weekly?

Briefly summarize what you need to do your best work with colleagues and what might get in the way.

_____

_____

_____

Know What You Need in a Manager

A manager who is committed to your learning and development can catalyze your career![12] Conversely, having a difficult manager can be unmotivating and disruptive to your job satisfaction and sense of well-being. It's particularly important to know what you need from your manager to do your best work; that clarity will greatly help you create a productive working relationship with your manager.

- Consider previous managers you've had: Who gave you the space and support to grow and learn? How did they engage with you? And what did you find helpful about their approach?

- How have you felt unsupported by past managers? What have been points of tension or conflict with managers in the past?

- What would you like to learn from your next manager? What type of expertise would you like your manager to have?

- How often do you like to meet with your manager? What would you like the structure and focus of those meetings to be?

- What style of management and leadership do you know definitely does and doesn't work for you?

---

12 A 2015 study looked at the relationship between employees and their managers through the lens of attachment theory—how individuals develop relationship attachments through repeated interactions. Crawshaw and Game found that the more effective managers were "aware of their employees' career needs and goals, were interpersonally accepting and understanding, could be easily approached for career support and advice, and worked collaboratively with their employees to facilitate their development aims" (p. 1197). Jonathan Crawshaw and Annilee Game, "The Role of Line Managers in Employee Career Management: An Attachment Theory Perspective," _The International Journal of Human Resource Management_, 26:9 (2015): 1182–1203. https://doi.org/10.1080/09585192.2014.934886.

What realizations have you had, if any? What are your top 3 needs in a manager in order of priority?

1. _____

2. _____

3. _____

Identify What You Want to Learn

Your next job is an opportunity to connect the skills and knowledge that you already have with new skills you want to develop in your career.

Regardless of whether your workplace offers learning opportunities, get clear on your personal learning goals. This might include formal learning like a course or certificate program or something more informal, such as reading on your own or seeking out a mentor. You may want to revisit your skills and experiences as well as your curiosities in chapter 4 as you think about what you want to learn in a new job.

What are your top three learning goals in your next job, in order of priority?

1. _____

2. _____

3. _____

Determine Your Target Salary and Benefits

Decisions regarding salary and benefits are very personal. They literally reflect your value in the job market and of course impact you and your family directly. In a number of US states, it's illegal to ask about salary history during an interview. The confidential nature of salaries in many workplaces perpetuates pay disparities, particularly for women, people of color, and other marginalized groups. You can do your part to make these systems more fair by taking a stand for the pay and benefits that you deserve—and also, when the time comes, advocating for those around you (more on this in chapter 10).

It can be especially difficult to prioritize your needs around salary, especially during an economic downturn. Yet we strongly recommend clarifying your target salary as you imagine job possibilities. You'll also want to be thoughtful about what benefits you need, such as health insurance, contributions to a retirement fund, flexibility, days off, student loan support, or equity in a company.

Important steps to gain clarity on your ideal salary and benefits include:

1. Establish an empowered mindset
Begin with your morning practice. Considering your feelings and needs, reflect on what salary range feels right. Decide on the specific dollar amount and the benefits you need, regardless of what you may think the market can offer. Now is the time to establish your ideal range. Later, you may have to make compromises during salary negotiations—more on that and the details of salary and benefits negotiation in chapter 9.

2. Do your homework
Use Glassdoor, LinkedIn, and other sites to do research on the salary ranges and benefits for the positions and organizations that you're interested in. Talk to friends and colleagues who might know what an appropriate salary and benefits range is for your experience level, role, and industry.

3. Determine your ideal salary and benefits
Find a happy medium between your ideal and the market rate,

considering your total benefits. If you find that your salary research and job postings show a lower rate than what you want, get clear on the low end of the salary range that is still energizing to you.

How much do you need and want to earn?

What benefits are must-haves (in order of priority)?

_____   _____

_____   _____

_____   _____

Decide to Freelance or Work Part-Time

As you spend time thinking about your ideal work, you may realize that you don't want a full-time job, but rather you want to work part-time or work more independently, running your own freelance business. Being a consultant or working part-time might work best with your optimal work-rest cycle and your current situation and allow you to most fully share your unique value.

Cathy has been working as an independent leadership coach and organizational development specialist for over twenty years. But, ironically, she never thought about having her own business until she was asked to write a career coaching column for Idealist.org. She soon realized there was an entirely different universe of work that was available to her after readers of her column asked her to set up coaching sessions!

Lauren's path to consulting was different. After becoming a coach, she was inspired by her mentors who ran successful businesses, so she started her own. This allowed her to build skills in coaching and organizational development. But after a year and a half, she craved a role on a team and more job stability. She decided to look for a full-time job, knowing that she could always return to consulting if she wanted to.

If you're feeling energized about working part-time or on your own, think about how you can pursue side projects while you're looking for a job, depending on your schedule. You may want to put together a rough business plan and share it with a friend or mentor.

Reflect on the following questions:
- Consider running every aspect of a business—from developing content to doing marketing and branding to managing finances. What feels energizing about it? What doubts arise?
- How would part-time or temporary work help you do your best work?

Is it optimal for you to look for a full-time job, a part-time job, or start your own business or consulting practice? Why?

_____

_____

_____

Test Out Your Ideal Work

Explore volunteer opportunities
As you explore what types of jobs might be a good fit, consider volunteering to learn about different work environments. One of Cathy's clients started as a volunteer in the ICU and decided to go to nursing school to become a nurse. In her case, volunteering literally changed her work life! Cathy has had many other clients who turned volunteering opportunities into jobs.

If you don't have a job, volunteering is a particularly great way to nourish yourself, remain engaged in the work world, and stay connected to others. The best way to find volunteer opportunities is to reach out to your community to see if they have the inside scoop on specific volunteer opportunities and organizations you might be interested in.

List any organizations or volunteer opportunities that you're interested in learning more about.

Create opportunities to shadow

Shadowing might involve observing a professional contact give a presentation on Zoom or asking a colleague to join a work session focused on a strategic initiative. Getting a glimpse of what people do and how they do it will accelerate your job search by providing an insider view of an organization or role. It's an immersive way to gather data about what it's really like to work in a particular sector, organization, and position. It will also activate your community as you get more exposure to other people in your network and learn more about what you want.

Having said this, we're surprised by how few formal opportunities exist for shadowing. You'll definitely need to find a strong advocate or someone who can serve as your host to make it happen! But it's well worth it, as it's one of the best ways to get a front-row seat to a job and imagine yourself in it, even if it's a virtual experience.

List any particular jobs you're interested in observing firsthand that would help you learn more about a particular role, organization, or sector.

Define Your Must-Haves and Deal Breakers

As you've gained clarity about the work you want to do, you'll want to develop what we call must-haves and deal breakers. What do you need to be in place to consider a job opportunity? We recommend using your list of must-haves and deal breakers as a litmus test as you decide what jobs to apply to and which ones you should pass on.

For instance, a must-have might be that you need a manager who likes to check in regularly with you on projects and is also supportive about personal development. A deal breaker might be that you want to stop working at 6 p.m., but you're willing to make an exception a few times a month. If a job description says that it requires you to be available around the clock, it's not the job for you!

Getting clear on your must-haves and deal breakers will help you discern where to put your energy in your search and will also inform your decision about whether to accept a job offer.

Identify and prioritize your top 3–5 must-haves.

1. _____
2. _____
3. _____
4. _____
5. _____

Identify and prioritize your top 3–5 deal breakers.

1. _____
2. _____
3. _____
4. _____
5. _____

Celebrate
AND
MAINTAIN
MOMENTUM

We know that we've given you a lot to sort through in this chapter. Hopefully you have a good sense of the type of roles you're interested in and also the industry and sectors, as well as a handful of organizations that appeal to you. Defining your ideal work is an ongoing process. Throughout your job search, you'll want to revisit and refine your must-haves and deal breakers. Next up: you'll continue to build a complete picture of your ideal work as you have connected conversations with your community.

Chapter 6

COMMUNITY BUILDING: MORE THAN NETWORKING

Get into a <u>CURIOUS</u> mindset

Map your community

Develop talking points

Reach out to your community

Have connected conversations

Manage your emotions when reaching out

Establish your Inspiration and Advisory Board

Stay connected with your community

Celebrate and maintain momentum

Abby, a self-described introvert in her late thirties, has always had a fraught relationship with networking. She's a people person—she enjoys being with colleagues and chatting about work, learning about their careers, and passing on helpful information. But parties, networking events, and the chore of "getting out there" exhaust her.

That was a real obstacle when she was looking for a new position at a boutique PR agency, after having spent the beginning of her career in a communications role at a tech company. Abby knew she needed to tap into her network to find a new role, but she hated the thought of selling herself

With coaching, Abby focused on clarifying and expressing her unique value. That, Cathy explained, was the key to understanding that her efforts to "get out there" weren't about selling herself, but rather learning about people and sharing her unique value. In that way, nurturing her network was about being more of herself, not less.

Furthermore, Abby had mentored quite a few people, and as a giver, she tended to be generous with her time. She started to realize that her outreach didn't have to feel transactional. As she became more comfortable reaching out to her community, she started to learn about opportunities, and in one of those conversations she learned about an open role, which ultimately led to a new job.

Many of you might feel like Abby does. Networking may evoke anxiety and feel inauthentic, as if you have to "sell yourself" and convince others of your value. That might give you hives.

We believe that it's much more effective and empowering to see networking through a different lens. Community building, as we call it, is a mutual process of exchange and discovery, where you intentionally share your unique value and ideal work while learning about others. In community building, you have connected conversations, not informational interviews. When you can tap into a sense of real connection to yourself and others, community building feels more genuine, collaborative, and energizing.[13]

Old Paradigm: Networking	New Paradigm: Community Building
You conduct informational interviews, focusing primarily on your needs.	You engage in connected conversations and mutual exploration, exploring both your needs and the other person's needs, which we call the virtuous cycle.
You prepare an "elevator pitch."	You prepare talking points about who you are and what your unique value is that you expand on and customize in the moment. This helps you share more of yourself and how you seek to contribute.
Your mantra is: I don't really have time to get to know you. I need a job.	Your mantra is: While I need a job, I own my power in the job search. I proceed with intention and care and understand that relationship building takes time.
You prioritize accumulating contacts, for example, adding anyone you meet on LinkedIn.	You prioritize quality over quantity, building a variety of meaningful relationships rooted in true connection.

---

13 Maslow includes love and belonging in his <u>hierarchy of needs.</u> Indeed, one of our strongest needs is to belong and feel connected to each other in meaningful ways. Baumeister & Leary (1995) suggest that frequent contact is needed to sustain relationships, the interactions need to be stable, ongoing, and involve mutual concern for each other. Roy Baumeister and Mark Leary. "The need to belong: desire for interpersonal attachments as a fundamental human motivation." Psychological bulletin 117, no. 3 (1995): 497, https://doi.org/10.1037/0033-2909.117.3.497.

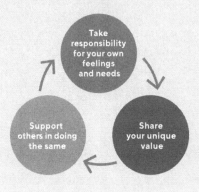

THE VIRTUOUS CYCLE

When you're in the virtuous cycle, you're able to balance your own feelings and needs with other peoples' feelings and needs, while always looking for ways to benefit each other. Possibilities and ideas emerge more organically. And you're ultimately able to contribute to better outcomes for everyone.[14]

Take responsibility for your own feelings and needs

Share your unique value

Support others in doing the same

Throughout this chapter, we'll show you how to deepen your community and embrace the virtuous cycle. We'll start by mapping out different levels of connection and how to have connected conversations. You'll clarify some of the key messages or talking points you'll want to share with your community. You'll discover new ways to step into your power and embrace connections that embody the virtuous cycle, while also managing your emotions as you reach out.

Get into a **CURIOUS** Mindset

Curiosity is one of the most powerful mindsets because it takes us out of our worries and into the present moment and something bigger than ourselves. It's a way we learn about the world and a helpful mindset to discover more about people and job possibilities.

---

14 MLK said in a speech in Montgomery, "Life's most persistent and urgent question is, 'What are you doing for others?'" Martin Luther King Jr., "Three Dimensions of a Complete Life" (speech, 1963).

Sometimes an idea or connection you have can lead to a new job, friendship, or even writing a book together! Getting curious about people, ideas, and jobs will help you stay open-minded as you reach out to your community. Reflecting on your feelings and needs can be particularly helpful to get into a curious mindset—it's a way of putting on your "oxygen mask" first so you can be more available to connect with others.

What initial questions, if any, do you have at this point about potential jobs, organizations, and people in your network?

_____

_____

Expressing gratitude for the people in your community is also a great way to set the stage for connected conversations and deepen your curiosity. You may want to incorporate more gratitude into your morning and evening practice when you're getting ready to dive into community building.

GRATITUDE PRACTICE FOR YOUR COMMUNITY

- Take a few minutes to sit quietly.
- Focus on your breathing and take deep belly-breaths, making sure that your exhale is longer than your inhale.
- Observe your thoughts and feelings, trying not to judge them.
- Acknowledge and name your feelings as they come up and let them go.
- Think about the people who have nurtured and supported you so far in your journey and those who have yet to appear.
- Think about all the people you have positively impacted or will positively impact through your work.
- Extend gratitude to them for the opportunity to know them, and wish them well on their journeys.

Map Your Community

Mapping your community can feel overwhelming if you have a lot of connections, or anxiety-provoking if you feel that you don't have enough. In both cases, be intentional about who you reach out to and when.

Ask yourself the following questions:
- Are you looking for advice?
- Do you need help clarifying the type of work you want to do?
- Are you hoping to talk to someone who has made a similar career leap or is familiar with the types of jobs you're considering?
- Do you need to learn more about specific roles?
- Are you hoping to connect with someone who works at a company you're interested in?

Knowing what's motivating you can help you be more grounded and clearer about what you're seeking when you connect with others. Below we share an approach that you can experiment with to map different layers of your community.

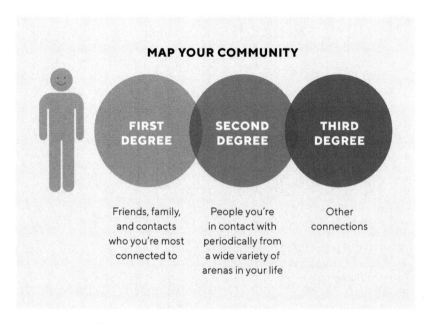

MAP YOUR COMMUNITY

FIRST DEGREE	SECOND DEGREE	THIRD DEGREE
Friends, family, and contacts who you're most connected to	People you're in contact with periodically from a wide variety of arenas in your life	Other connections

Your first degree connections consist of friends, family, and contacts who you're most connected to and comfortable with. Your besties. Your A-team. Your VIPs! In chapter 1, we encouraged you to establish a team to support you through this journey. You might turn to these individuals for encouragement and potential introductions—they care about you and are likely to know of opportunities that might help you. Lauren likes to jokingly refer to this as the "Mom and Pop Network." Often our clients assume that these contacts need to be in the field that they're interested in, but that isn't the case! They might have little or no connection to your field or sector but know people who do.

Your second degree connections consist of people you're in contact with somewhat regularly from a wide variety of arenas in your life, who you aren't as close to as your first degree connections. These may be professional contacts you've maintained relationships with or someone you met at a conference. What's important is that they're a part of your extended community and may help you understand the landscape for a sector or job function you're considering and know of relevant opportunities. It's often helpful to review the list of organizations you're interested in (that you created in chapter 5) and try to connect with people who work there.

Your third degree connections represent the rest of your community, including people you haven't talked to in ages, thought leaders you follow, and more distant connections.

As you think about your community, look out for super connectors, or, as Malcom Gladwell calls them, "mavens". Mavens are people who love to connect people to each other in meaningful ways. These connectors are key to your job search. They make the time to have engaged conversations with you. Having a few mavens in your community can be a game-changer! And don't worry if you don't have any yet—you'll likely encounter them over time.

At the same time, know that your degrees of connection are fluid. They regularly shift and change. You might find that someone who was a third degree connection for many years, through conversations about your kids and parenting, becomes a second degree connection and a steady presence in your life.

Develop Talking Points

Talking points provide a tangible way to share your unique value and ideal work with the world! They are a flexible set of messages to help you connect with your community. You can also use your talking points to inform your résumé and cover letters, prepare for interviews, or add nuance and detail to your social media profiles on LinkedIn, for example.

When you're actually sharing your talking points, you'll likely add in vivid details and explain what you mean by, for example, "leadership development" and "mission-driven organizations." Avoid generic buzzwords or language like *"I want to make an impact," "I want to work on a great team,"* or *"I want to do meaningful work."* Instead, go deeper to define what you mean and paint a detailed but succinct picture, using metaphors or imagery when possible.

By taking the time to define your talking points, you'll be more likely to stay connected to your power instead of struggling to figure out what your goals are for the conversation and what to share in the moment. And don't worry about your audience—at first. Follow the four steps below and frame your talking points in a way that works for you.

1. Review and summarize your unique value and ideal work
Review your unique value and your ideal work from the last two chapters. Given the opportunities you're considering, choose what you're most excited to share. For example, you might highlight your skills, ideas, and passions and what types of positions you're considering.

2. Find a frame that works

There is no one right way to share your talking points! We really mean it. We understand that that could feel both liberating and overwhelming. We offer a few different ways to frame your talking points to give you a starting point.

3. Share and revise

Practice sharing your talking points with a friend, coach, or colleague, and get feedback. Revise and practice them until you feel energized about what you're going to share.

4. Customize your talking points

Once you have your core messages, you'll be able to tweak what you share for different contexts. For example, when Lauren was recently looking for a job, she was open to positions in the nonprofit and philanthropy space, as well as opportunities in the tech world. Knowing her unique value in depth and variations on her ideal work helped her develop a set of talking points that she was able to customize depending on the conversation.

EXAMPLE FRAMES

Career story highlighting skills

A somewhat traditional approach, it focuses on framing your unique value and ideal work within the context of your larger goals and career arc—the summary of how you got to where you are now in your career.

I am a _____ with __ years of experience doing _____ (skills, experiences) for _____ (types of organizations you've worked in). I'm proud of having created _____ (accomplishments). I'm excited to find a role that will allow me to share my _____ (expertise/unique value) at _____ (organizational culture/mission).

Lauren's example: *I'm a management consultant turned talent/learning professional. I spent the first seven years of my career working on projects ranging from strategy to operations to leadership development. In the past seven years, I've focused most on leadership, learning and coaching as I seek to empower people in the work world. I've developed management and leadership development programs that help build leaders' self-awareness, using a cohort-based model. I have a passion for helping people navigate their career paths and giving them the tools to succeed on and off the job. While I've primarily worked in the social sector, I'm excited to find a role where I can design learning and leadership development in a forward-thinking company.*

Narrative or story based

This approach highlights a pivotal moment in your personal and/ or professional life, or an epiphany you had and how it's impacted what you want to pursue. Sometimes it's helpful to use this frame when you want advice on how to incorporate your interests and/ or passions into a viable job opportunity.

I had a transformational experience when I _____ (name the experience and/or moment). It changed the way that I saw myself and my work. I realized that I want to _____ (talk about the impact you want to make in the world).

Example: *I spent a few months traveling in Southeast Asia and was inspired by the amazing women I met who were selling their beautiful artwork. I'm feeling really energized about working in international development and being part of a mission-driven organization where I can empower girls and women. For example, I could see myself developing similar programs for a nonprofit or NGO located in the US.*

Ideas focus

If you have a clear sense of your ideal work, you may want to lead with your big ideas. As you connect with your community, you can test out your ideas and see if it's possible to transform them into concrete opportunities. This frame also works well if you're looking for ways to contribute to short-term projects or if you're exploring a business idea.

I'm really excited about _____ (insert the idea). I could see it working in _____ (share some of the ways you've been thinking about executing your strategy). I'm really suited for this type of work because of my _____ (share specific skills and experiences given your unique value you bring).

Example: *I'm passionate about creating short animated videos on new technology. I could see myself working for a production company or even joining an internal communications team. My background in journalism and my experience working for a local television production company give me a strong understanding of narrative. I've also spent the past year growing my skills in video editing in 3D animation and producing short YouTube videos.*

Reach Out to Your Community

Start reaching out to your first degree connections because they're typically the easiest people to approach and will help you build your ease and confidence. As you continue your job search, try contacting 1–3 people and/or organizations per week in a purposeful way. Connecting with fewer people might not give you enough momentum and reaching out to more might be hard to manage as you set up meetings.

Write down 10–20 people you would like to connect with over the next few months. We recommend creating a way to organize your connections with a community outreach tracker in whatever form works best for you. If it's useful to you, you may want to note the level of connection. At the same time, it's often helpful to list contacts from the organizations you're interested in (from chapter 5) and others that you learn about as you reach out to your community. You can incorporate these contacts into your community outreach tracker.

COMMUNITY OUTREACH TRACKER

NAME	DEGREE OF CONNECTION	TITLE, ORGANIZATION	WHY YOU'RE INTERESTED IN CONNECTING	DATE OF MEETING	FOLLOW-UP AND INSIGHTS

If you've just been laid off or you don't yet have a clear sense of what you want to do next, you may want to pause on your community building for a few days or even weeks. We've seen that doing so can actually expedite your search, because it allows you the space to connect to yourself and clarify key aspects of what you are and aren't looking for. You can then connect with your community at another time when you're feeling more energized and focused.

Outreach Emails

An outreach email can take multiple forms. You may choose to reach out to a first, second, or third degree connection directly or you may ask someone in your network to make an introduction. How much you share will depend on your relationship and the context. You need to be clear about what you're looking for help or advice on. Make your ask up front and share a version of your talking points. It may be helpful to create a 3–5 paragraph email with your goals in mind and edit it based on who you're reaching out to.

Sending an outreach email

SUBJECT: Scheduling a time to catch up

Hi Dara,

How are you doing? We connected a few years ago and your name recently came up in a conversation. I was excited to hear that you recently started a new job and I would love to hear more about it. Would you be open to a short conversation in the next few weeks?

A bit more about what I've been up to: I'm currently in an executive master's and doctoral program at Penn in organizational leadership and learning. I also work at a professional services firm where I focus on nonprofit executive director search, leadership development, and succession planning. I am eager to dig my heels into a new opportunity focused on internal talent/people/learning and development.

I'm eager to hear what you're up to, and I could certainly use some advice as I pivot my career (while working full-time, being in school part-time, and being a mother of a toddler)!

Thanks,
Lauren

Have Connected Conversations

We think the term "informational interviews" is problematic because it perpetuates the old paradigm of being transactional or one-sided as you connect with your community. As we've discussed, we prefer to use the term *connected conversations* as an opportunity to exchange information *and* build relationship.

Connected conversations are the essence of the new paradigm of community building—sharing your unique value and engaging others—and they are fundamental to the virtuous cycle.

These conversations will help you learn more about specific jobs titles, organizations, and sectors. They give you the opportunity to ask questions like, *"What do you think I'm missing in my experience to get this type of job?"* or *"Are there any people or organizations that you think I should connect with?"* Within about a month of having multiple connected conversations, you'll notice that you've deepened your relationships and have a better sense of the fields you're interested in and what possibilities exist.

During connected conversations, focus on how you listen and respond. Even the best communicators and the most self-aware can benefit by reflecting on how to listen on a deeper level and more easily enter into the virtuous cycle. Pay attention to what you're feeling, needing, and sharing and really consider what the other person is feeling, needing, and sharing.

WAYS TO LISTEN IN CONNECTED CONVERSATIONS

Listening Mode	How to Listen and Respond
Advice Seeking	Directly ask for specific advice and brainstorm possibilities together. Listen attentively and ask clarifying questions. Ask permission when requesting advice, as not everyone will want to give it. Similarly, if you're in the mode of advice giver, we recommend asking permission before offering advice!
Informational Listening	Gather data and information to problem-solve and build knowledge. Ask lots of questions.
Reflective Listening	Listen without an agenda, giving the speaker space to share their thoughts and ideas. Wait for the other person to complete what they're sharing without responding in the moment. Reflect back on the main points you heard and ask if you understood correctly.
Silent Listening	Remain mostly quiet to give the speaker time to share their experience and fully absorb what they're saying. Nod, but resist offering verbal affirmation.

How do you tend to listen in conversations? What do you want to do more or less of?

_____

_____

_____

You'll want to prepare 5-10 questions for your connected conversations. Try to do more reflective and silent listening and also experiment with modes that you don't use as often.

Keep in mind the following:

- Align the tone and structure of your meetings with the context of your relationship. For example, if you already know the person well, you're likely to be more casual and maybe share more questions than you might with a new connection.
- We suggest that you use whatever communication style works best for both of you to have a conversation—whether it's a text exchange, email, 20-minute phone conversation, or an in-person meeting.
- Schedule up to three conversations per week so you keep momentum, but also give yourself enough time to prepare and follow up.

AN EXAMPLE OF A CONNECTED CONVERSATION

Path and Background

Start by sharing a customized version of your talking points, highlighting your unique value and what you're looking for in your next job. Then go with the flow of the conversation and ask:

- Can you tell me more about your background and what led you to where you are now?
- In hindsight, what would you do differently to get where you are?

Get really clear on your questions before going into the conversation, and don't forget—you're in the virtuous cycle, so you'll also want to engage in a way that feels mutual.

- What does your role entail? What does an average workday look like?
- What do you love most and least about your job or company?
- Can you tell me more about your team and how it is structured?
- Who do you think are some of the top leaders in this field/sector?
- Where is hiring occurring—in what sectors/organizations/types of positions? What is being funded?

Next Steps/Ideas and Insight

Express gratitude and any immediate takeaways and insights from the conversation. Send a thank you note soon after. Follow up on any commitments made during the conversation or share any relevant articles or resources you discussed.

- Are there specific skills you think I should be developing?
- Who might you recommend that I connect with?
- What do you think would be useful for me to read or pay attention to?
- Would you be willing to share jobs that seem like a good fit based on what I've shared?
- No pressure at all, but would you consider having me shadow you in an upcoming meeting or workshop you're leading?

Manage Your Emotions When Reaching Out

You are likely to experience many emotions when you reach out to your community. If you're embarrassed or anxious about needing to turn to others for support or you haven't been in touch with someone recently, remind yourself that it's normal to ask for help and feel these emotions.

THE FRONT DOOR FORMULA
Sort through feedback at the "front door"

We often think of setting boundaries as what we say yes to and no to with other people, but it can often be with *ourselves*. When you're community building, sometimes people offer suggestions and ideas that are illuminating and helpful; you can easily say yes to them. But other times, their recommendations may be less helpful. We refer to the process of sorting through this feedback as the *front door formula*, because metaphorically you can decide what you want to leave at the front door and what you want to bring inside. Actively *choose* what to do with feedback—consider it without becoming either overly attached to it or dismissing it.

At times, being specific about what feedback you are and aren't looking for can alleviate tricky situations. Those closest to us can sometimes overstep or give advice on something we're not looking for. It's useful to have a few phrases at the ready to keep the conversation on track. *"I imagine that you really want to be supportive. What helps me the most is when you listen rather than provide advice. Additionally, I would be so grateful if you didn't share your anxiety about my not having a job yet and instead ask me what I need."* When you're clear about the type of support you need, you will feel more empowered and maintain your momentum.

If you've lost a job, you may feel grief or sadness and find yourself reliving the experience when people ask what you've been doing recently. Going back to the Emotional Breakthrough Process during these times can be helpful. Additionally, gratitude and getting present may help you as you tap into your feelings and needs and turn to your community for support, not away from it.

As we've discussed earlier in the chapter, when you're coming from a place of genuine curiosity, there is a mutuality in reaching out, even when you're connecting with second and third degree connections and you haven't been in touch for a while. It's okay to say, *"I've been remiss about being in touch, and I would love to catch up."*

What emotions are present for you as you reach out to people in your community? What strategies do you plan to use to manage your emotions as you reach out?

_____

_____

Establish an Inspiration and Advisory Board

Many of our clients have benefited greatly from having an advisory board that not only includes advocates and mentors they know personally, but also experts in their field and other sources of inspiration whose writings or even artwork guide them.

Think about who and what helps you feel connected to yourself and your community and, indeed, inspired! She has Sharon Salzberg, Cheryl Strayed, and Seth Godin on her board. Lauren sometimes asks herself when she's embarking on a new project: "What would Seth Godin do?" Not surprisingly, many of our clients have Brene Brown on their board. You may even want to consider deceased individuals whose wisdom, words, and work energize you and that you can access at any point in time.

CATHY'S INSPIRATION AND ADVISORY BOARD

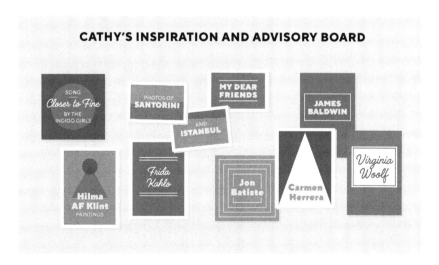

Set Up Your Inspiration and Advisory Board:

- Select 5–10 "members" that inspire and encourage you, reflecting on the support and inspiration that would be the most helpful to you.
- Check in with one of your members, if you can, once a week; that might be giving a mentor a call or reading a blog post. Continually discern whether it's helpful to set up meetings with members or draw wisdom from their words or creations.
- Always be on the hunt for new board members even as you maintain a vibrant connection to current ones.

List who and what is on your Inspiration and Advisory Board.

_____

_____

Stay Connected with Your Community

"Dunbar's number" or the "rule of 150" proposes that most people can only maintain up to 150 relationships on average at any given time, including family, friends, and professional contacts.[15] We believe that it's up to you to clarify what types of relationships and how many you want to build over time. For example, some of you might do best when you're connected with a smaller group of fewer than 50 connections, and others may do better with more than 150.

Reflect on what really allows you to stay connected with your community, given your personality and particular needs and goals.

_____

15 Research on personal social networks suggests three layers of network size—an innermost layer with fewer than 5 members; another layer of up to 24 members who are in touch monthly. The third layer of the network size is around 136–150 contacts, close to what Dunbar predicted for humans based on his research studying nonhuman primates' brains and group sizes. This active network includes contacts who have been in touch within the past two years. Note that this research study only included self-identifying females. Sam Roberts, Robin Dunbar, Thomas Pollet and Toon Kuppens. "Exploring Variation in Active Network Size: Constraints and Ego Characteristics," _Social Network_ 31, no. 2 (2009): 138-146, https://doi.org/10.1016/j.socnet.2008.12.002.

A number of our clients often ask how often is it best to be in touch with their connections. Generally, we recommend being in touch with your entire community about twice a year, if possible, whether you're in a job search or not. Of course, there will be some people in your network that you might be in touch with weekly or even daily, depending on your relationship.

Overall, it's optimal to find ways to engage with your community that feel authentic, whether that is offering a note of congratulations when someone gets a promotion or changes jobs or commenting on someone's blog post or recent publication. You might send an occasional email or text that says something like, *"I was thinking of you and wanted to check in to see how you're doing."* Some of our clients send annual holiday cards or email updates, which help maintain their connections. Whatever you decide to do, keep your community posted on important milestones in your life.

In what ways do you want to be intentional about staying connected to your community? Who do you want to be in regular touch with and how often?

You've started the deep work of nurturing your community and putting structures in place that will reap benefits for years to come. Pause and celebrate what a generous community you have! As you turn your attention to preparing your application materials in the next chapter, don't forget to keep calling on your community from your Inspiration and Advisory Board to your colleagues and friends. Remind yourself of the power of the virtuous cycle even in the midst of honing the details of your résumé and cover letter.

Chapter 7

APPLY!

Get into a <u>DISCIPLINED</u> mindset

Establish and maintain your online presence

Where to look for jobs

Apply for jobs

Reimagine your résumé

Create a one-of-a-kind cover letter

Choose your references wisely

Write your own work proposal

How to deal with your emotions
if you don't hear back

Celebrate and maintain momentum

Yasmin

GETS
MOTIVATED

Yasmin, a forty-five-year-old educational consultant, was hoping to move to the classroom. She was in the process of leaving her job when the pandemic began. Just my luck, she told Cathy, her coach, only half joking. She finally had clarity on her ideal job: being a teacher and working with students day in and day out; not just advising administrators and focusing on high-level education policy.

But when it was time to start actually applying for jobs, Yasmin felt unmotivated. Although she had already done a lot of work clarifying her unique value and ideal work, it felt like editing her résumé and creating cover letters was a heavy lift, on top of the stress she was experiencing in her day job and being a mother of three. Yasmin was also frustrated that each school district had a different process to apply, and she knew that she needed to get her application materials in soon to be eligible for the upcoming school year.

Working with Cathy, she started to realize that she had already done a lot of the work that she needed to start applying for specific openings at schools. By identifying that she wanted to be back in the classroom, Yasmin also had articulated her talking points. Now she just needed to make the time to translate those talking points into a cover letter and updated résumé. For a couple of weeks, she carved out a few hours after her kids went to sleep, and she took a couple of short breaks throughout her workday to get some fresh air and reinvigorate herself amid homeschooling and working. This helped her stay positive and focused.

The moment has arrived. It's finally time to take everything you've been working on and focus on actively applying for jobs. If you've taken the important steps in the previous chapters of getting in touch with your feelings and needs, connecting to your unique value, defining your ideal work, and building community, you're in a strong position to navigate this sometimes dreaded part of the job search from an empowered place.

In this chapter, we go deep into the application process, outlining a new paradigm for résumés and cover letters. You'll learn how to share more about yourself in your materials by leading with your unique value. We also share examples to guide your search. By the end of this chapter, we hope that you'll have all your application materials ready as you identify job opportunities that you want to apply for!

Get into a <u>DISCIPLINED</u> Mindset

At this point, you may feel like you've already climbed a number of mountains. And there are still more to traverse as you find ways to translate your unique value and ideal work into your application materials in succinct, engaging ways. That's why having a disciplined mindset—following through on your goals and commitments daily—will help you at this stage in the process.

Take a moment to reflect on how disciplined and focused you've already been by reading this book and (hopefully) engaging with your morning and evening practices and the breakthrough process. It can take up to four to six weeks to hear back on an initial application, so staying disciplined will help you immensely. Make sure that you're sticking to your daily practices and the structures you set up to guide your search, as you continue to build your discipline and concentration.

On a scale of 1–10 (with 10 being the most disciplined), how disciplined are you at this point in the search? What are 1–2 small shifts you can make in your morning or evening practice and/or throughout the day to increase your discipline?

_____

_____

Establish and Maintain Your Online Presence

Before you start applying for jobs, take the time to update your online presence. It's no longer seen as a signal that you're looking for a new job, but rather is part of having good social media hygiene. It's usually easiest to update your social media at the same time as you work on your applications to make sure your online presence is consistent with the rest of your materials. And don't forget to google yourself, to see what a potential employer might learn about you!

You'll want to decide which sites you want to regularly update. Be authentic and engage with social media in a way that reflects how you seek to contribute to your professional community. Updating your social media requires a good deal of work, so get clear on what you really have the energy for. It can be helpful to set weekly or monthly reminders to update them.

At a minimum, we recommend maintaining a vibrant LinkedIn profile when you're looking for a job. You might also want to think about a broader social media strategy that includes Twitter, Instagram, or TikTok. Potential employers will likely look you up online to gauge your credibility and understand your skills and experiences beyond any materials you've submitted.

Below are recommendations for your LinkedIn profile, which you can also consider for other social media platforms.

Headline

We often get asked whether your headline in LinkedIn should be your job title or if it's okay to use other descriptors. While there is no one right way, ensure that your headline is accurate and clear. Experiment with what feels most aligned for you! You might choose to use your title and organization because it describes your work best or it may be important for you professionally. You can also use creative headlines such as "Author," "Connector," or "Entrepreneur." Look at other profiles of people you admire who work in a similar field to get inspired.

Summary and profile

You'll want to incorporate the talking points that you developed in chapter 6 and language from your résumé, particularly if you're writing a summary of expertise or a headline at the top of your résumé. Some of our clients like to tell a story or pose questions in their summary to showcase their unique value and share examples of work products.

Recommendations

Having 5–15 testimonials, or recommendations, will help to paint a fuller picture of how you've contributed in the past and what you're capable of. If you're comfortable, invite people to share a particular aspect of your work so you can shape a larger (composite) narrative that highlights your unique value.

Sharing articles and writing posts

If you're looking to switch sectors or industries, it can be particularly helpful to document what you're learning with your community. A simple way to do that is to share articles or write posts that are relevant to the work you're looking to do. We recommend posting substantive content at least once a month when you're actively looking for a job.

Where to Look for Jobs

As you have connected conversations, specific opportunities will surface as people send you jobs and connect you with people in the know about your industry/sector. This is often the best way to learn about relevant job opportunities and is a byproduct of effective community building. At the same time, you'll want to do research on your own, looking to organization's websites, industry sites, job boards and social media.

Organizations' websites

Remember that list of organizations you worked on in chapter 5? You'll want to go directly to their websites and social media to learn about open positions. If you're directly connected to the company or you have a connection with someone working there, start with a conversation regardless of whether there's a current job opportunity that looks like a good fit. A conversation might open the door for a position in the future that may not exist right now. And if there is an open position, do your best to connect with the hiring manager or your contact to learn more before you apply, if possible.

Job listings and social media

This is a great way to get ideas about jobs, but not always the best way to find them. LinkedIn and other sites such as Idealist and Glassdoor make it simple to apply for a job. Recruiters and hiring managers tell us that these applications can often feel generic and need more context. If there's another way to apply for a job through an organization's own website, for example, we recommend that.

Industry sites

Following industry experts or analysts, reading up on industry trends and learning more about related associations are great ways to learn about specific job opportunities. Many industrywide newsletters and sites aggregate job openings. For example, if you're looking for jobs in philanthropy, you'd want to visit the Chronicle of Philanthropy, Council on Foundations, Grantmakers for Effective Organizations, and Bridgespan. When you're staying on top of industry trends via a newsletter or social media, you're more likely to get clued in to who's currently hiring.

GET THROUGH THE BOTS

As you likely know, many organizations use applicant tracking systems to more easily identify top candidates. A lot of companies are also experimenting with artificial intelligence to identify potential candidates and also to diversify their candidate pools. A lot of these technologies don't necessarily make the application or interview process easier, and in some cases, they may even be harming the process—i.e., perpetuating an unconscious bias and missing out on top talent. In these software systems, using key terms or phrases is crucial, as they increase your likelihood of getting noticed.

Apply for Jobs

As we've mentioned, putting together a thoughtful application can take several hours or even a few days. So you'll need to decide whether it's worth your time and energy to apply. Typically, it's optimal to apply for one to three jobs per week. Once you've done it a few times, the process gets significantly faster.

As you consider new opportunities, continuously evaluate whether the positions you're interested in match your ideal work and values.

Prioritize your fit with a job over the quantity of applications you submit.

Even if you apply to a job you're really excited about, continue to look for other opportunities so you're not putting all your energy into one option. To decide whether you really want to put the time and effort into applying for a job, review the following questions:

Your Energy and Excitement about the Role

- How energized are you about the position (including the daily activities, salary and benefits, etc.)? In our experience, if you're not at least about a 7 out of 10 (10 being the most energized), you may want to reconsider whether it's worth applying.
- How energized are you about the organization (including mission, culture, decision-making, etc.)? Again, if you're not at least a 7 out of 10, consider what you might be compromising.
- Are you daydreaming about what your day-to-day might entail and/or getting new ideas related to the role?

Your Unique Value, Must-Haves, and Deal Breakers

- To what degree do you think you will be able to share your unique value? If you're at least a 7 out of 10, it's likely worth applying.
- Does your work experience meet at least 80 percent of the job qualifications, or do you have transferable skills where you're missing key experience? If not, consider whether it's worth it to apply. If you have a strong gut reaction that you should apply even if you don't meet 80 percent of the qualifications, go for it!
- How does the job match up to your list of must-haves and deal breakers in chapter 5? Ideally, the role should meet the majority of or at least your top three must-haves and deal breakers.

Reimagine Your Résumé

Who wants to read a dull résumé?! We're actually surprised that résumé structures haven't shifted more dramatically and that traditional versions still persist. The good news is that employers are increasingly open to more creative and longer formats for résumés. This gives you more space to share your narrative in a way that truly reflects the depth and breadth of your gifts and experience. And because there's no one way to write a résumé, you really can make it your own.

Old Paradigm	New Paradigm
You focus on **selling** yourself and convincing the organization of your value.	You focus on **sharing** yourself and helping the organization see how you can contribute.
Your résumé reads as a laundry list of jobs and responsibilities, without using enough specific language that communicates your unique value.	You showcase the impact you've made and what your specific role was. You describe how you've made a difference by creating products, processes, structures, systems, and building relationships.
You have numerous versions of your résumé because you start from the premise that you need to adapt yourself to different audiences.	You have one main version of your résumé that's grounded in your unique value. You lightly tweak it based on the nuance of the position and the organization.
Your résumé is one page because you need to convince a hiring manager of your worth quickly.	You aren't limited to a one-page résumé. You take the space you need to explain your story and highlight your unique value, while still being succinct.
You use a standard template.	You experiment with different ways of organizing your résumé and communicating your unique value in creative ways.
You stick with traditional résumé categories.	You consider adding sections to your résumé such as "Cross-Cultural Experience" and showcase unique hobbies or passions that may not be directly connected to your career arc but demonstrate your skills and experiences in other ways.

We've had clients who include less traditional choices such as quotes, images, or interactive elements online. Experiment with these and have, dare we say, a little bit of fun if they feel aligned with your style and your story. Just be sure that your résumé choices reflect expectations in your industry.

Don't waste your energy trying to figure out what a particular hiring manager prefers. Everyone's opinion is different. It's better to focus on making sure that your unique value comes through clearly in your résumé.

How Do I Get Started?

Start by creating what we call a back-office résumé, an unedited laundry list that details your complete work history. It's similar to a traditional curriculum vitae or CV, but even more extensive. This is a helpful way to take stock of all of your accomplishments and experiences so you can choose what you want to showcase in your actual résumé. You won't necessarily share this with anyone; rather, it's a way to be thorough and organized.

Another way to get into the résumé-writing flow is to develop what Cathy calls the inner psyche résumé. It's a version of your résumé that not only reflects your skills and experiences but also the emotional impact of your work on you and others. This is also a version that you will likely not show anyone, except a friend, career coach, or close colleague, but it's important because it allows you to unpack some of the underlying feelings and needs in your career. The inner psyche résumé will help you start to tease out what feels most authentic and engaging to share in your actual résumé.

Be prepared to spend several hours or even a few days revisiting and refining your résumé.

If you're feeling stuck or want to kickstart your creativity, experiment with what works best for you. It might be helpful to review older versions of your résumé or start brainstorming right away using the work you did on your unique value.

HOW THE INNER PSYCHE RÉSUMÉ CAN HELP YOU

Accomplishment

I wrote three grant proposals of $500,000 and was awarded unrestricted funding from three foundations.

Inner Psyche response
Examine the feelings behind a specific accomplishment.

I was feeling insecure since I had never written a grant proposal, but I really honed my writing skills and talked to the CEO to better understand why we needed to make this ask. When we received the funding, I felt so proud.

How this helps you

Knowing how you felt and how you overcame obstacles will help you communicate your strengths and your particular role in achieving a goal. Moreover, it's likely to give you information on creative strategies you can use to work through challenges.

In the following examples, you'll see an abbreviated version of Lauren's résumé as well as a modified client example with some tips to consider as you work on yours.

EXAMPLE RÉSUMÉ #1

Lauren Weinstein
Phone Number · Email · Washington, DC

I empower individuals, teams, and organizations to thrive in their work and in the world.

Lauren chose to use a short tagline/mission statement, because it felt authentic to her communication style. In earlier drafts of her résumé, she tried to put together a longer summary of expertise, but it felt too repetitive and jargony.

WORK EXPERIENCE

Degreed
Director, Learning and Development – Virtual
July 2020–Present

I lead internal learning and development for Degreed's 500+ employees, balancing our learning and skill strategy with business needs and ongoing product development.

- I mobilized a cross-functional team to revamp and relaunch Degreed internally (our own learning and upskilling platform).
- I'm developing a learning series and resources for managers.

Even when Lauren wasn't in her job for long, she started to add bullets, as she knows that it's important to continuously keep her résumé up-to-date and to do so when the information is fresh.

Depending on your skills and experiences, identify 3–5 major subject headings that you need to accurately reflect your experience and to serve as an overarching structure for your résumé. Lauren felt that in addition to her work experience, it was important to highlight her credentials and showcase her coaching experience.

Examples of categories include:

- Volunteer Experience
- Speaking Experience
- Publications
- Languages and International Experience

- Artistic Experience
- Continuing Education/Trainings and Certifications
- Education

Raffa-Marcum's Nonprofit and Social Sector Group
Manager – Washington, DC
Sept 2019–July 2020
Supervisor – Washington, DC
Jan 2019–Aug 2019
Senior Associate – Washington, DC
Dec 2017–Dec 2018

I worked with nonprofit boards and search committees to lead executive searches and succession planning. I also designed and facilitated leadership programs and workshops.

- I led dozens of searches, resulting in 16 executive-level hires at mission-driven organizations. I coached departing executives and newly hired executives to ensure successful transitions.
- For HIAS, an international humanitarian nonprofit, I created and facilitated a virtual leadership program for country directors overseeing 550+ staff.

Charles and Lynn Schusterman Family Foundation
Program Officer for Talent – Washington, DC
April 2015–Dec 2017

As a member of the senior leadership team, I set the strategic direction for the CareerHub platform and identified new talent solutions for the Jewish nonprofit sector. I advised grantees on hiring and coached hundreds of individuals, helping 40 people get new jobs.

- I designed, prototyped, and launched CareerHub, a technology platform to recruit top talent into the Jewish nonprofit sector, reaching more than 1,200 unique visitors/month.
- I co-developed and co-facilitated CareerLeap, a six-month career leadership program that included a two-day in-person workshop, virtual learning, and 1:1 coaching.
- I advised more than 30 grantees and partner organizations on talent and hiring strategies, enhancing employee engagement.

Use accurate and strong action verbs (e.g., designed, launched, or created) and be as specific as possible about who, what, where, and how much.

Coachable LLC
Consultant and Coach – Washington, DC
Oct 2013–March 2015

I ran my own coaching and consulting business working with small- and medium-sized businesses, nonprofits, and NGOs focused on strategy and organizational development.

- As a trainer and sales rep for More Than Money Careers, I led 12 training sessions on careers in social impact at six universities for over 500 undergraduate and graduate students. I also ran product demos and signed on universities as clients.
- For PresenTense (now Upstart), I led six trainings for entrepreneurs participating in an accelerator with a focus on design thinking.

Put the dates of when you worked in a specific job on the right-hand side of your résumé (as shown in the thumbnail above). Lauren felt it was important to include the months to show how each subsequent job flowed into the other, as part of her broader career narrative.

Accenture
Sept 2006–Sept 2013

As a management consultant, I worked with for-profit and nonprofit clients on strategy, operations, process improvement, technology initiatives, and leadership development.

Manager – Washington, DC; Brazil; India; Switzerland; Thailand
Sept 2011–Sept 2013

- I co-developed a competency model and approach for the International Rescue Committee's global management development program for 400 managers.
- Serving as faculty at Accenture's global training center, I spent 80 hours teaching management consulting skills and case studies to new Accenture employees.
- I designed and launched the Womanity Award to combat violence against women after conducting research in Brazil, India, Switzerland, and Thailand.
- Overseeing a team of three consultants, I built partnerships with nonprofits and health insurers to increase access to patient navigation.

When you've had multiple positions at the same organization, put the name of the organization first. However, if you haven't, putting your title first makes it easier for a reader to follow your career's evolution.

Consultant – Washington, DC; England; Mexico; India
Sept 2008–Aug 2011

- I co-developed a new operating model and global strategy for the World Association of Girl Guides and Girl Scouts after conducting research at global leadership centers.
- I did business development for Accenture Development Partnerships, including writing proposals and staffing over 40 employees for international development projects.

Analyst – Philadelphia, PA; Brazil; India
Sept 2006–Aug 2008

- I managed ten-person technology teams in Brazil and India testing a health website.
- I helped to expand Accenture's corporate social responsibility programs in the US and engaged hundreds of employees via a volunteer platform.

LANGUAGES
Spanish (fluent); Portuguese and Hebrew (beginner)

COACHING CREDENTIALS AND CONTINUING EDUCATION
- Associate Certified Coach (ACC), International Coach Federation, 2018
- Georgetown University Certification in Leadership Coaching, 2013

EDUCATION
Executive Master's and Doctorate in Organizational Leadership and Learning, 2022
Graduate School of Education, University of Pennsylvania

BA Communication, 2006
Annenberg School for Communication, University of Pennsylvania

- Varsity Swim Team, Captain

Even though work is becoming more virtual, it's still helpful to include the location of your job in your résumé. In this case, Lauren wanted to showcase that she had worked in different cultural and global contexts.

Get up to two people to review your résumé and provide feedback to you. Make sure that your résumé feels aligned with your gut, no matter what feedback you get.

If you're including an academic credential, discern how detailed you want to be. Here, Lauren mentions "Annenberg" because the communication program is known nationwide but leaves out her minor because it's not as relevant.

EXAMPLE RÉSUMÉ #2

Donda K.

Email / Phone Number / Location

Include your contact information so that it is easily accessible. You don't have to include your full address; rather note your city or town.

SUMMARY OF EXPERTISE

I am a vibrant, warm leader, and I am passionate about activating people to bring their fullest selves to their work. With over 20 years of experience across the nonprofit, corporate, and entrepreneurial sectors, I bring a unique blend of legal experience and an expansive, heart-centered consciousness with a focus on operations, communications, human resources, and fundraising. Throughout my work, I practice a facilitative leadership style geared toward maximizing collaboration. I am committed to learning and growing with others to help make our world better. Selected career accomplishments include:

Select a résumé format that highlights your unique value, strengths, and style. In Donna's case, she decided to showcase her unique value in a "Summary of Expertise" as an alternate option to a tagline.

Implementing systems and strategy

- I maximize individual and team contributions by bringing complex information and processes to life, making them accessible for a wide range of staff.
- At Rethink Environment, I develop project management tools that helps the team prioritize work and track progress on key projects, resulting in increased morale and more effective collaboration.

If you use subjective language like "warm" or "vibrant," make sure that you provide concrete examples, either in the rest of your Summary of Expertise or in the body of your résumé. No matter what, choose language that feels authentic to you.

Maximizing communication

- I align messaging with core institutional values, expand brand awareness, increase program participation, and meet and exceed fundraising and earned revenue goals.

- I partnered with the development department at Centered Retreat Center to successfully launch a year-end giving campaign that raised more than $500,000 and brought in ten new large donors.

Building and strengthening talent

- From hiring through performance evaluation, I aim to gain a deep understanding of what motivates people so they can be empowered to bring forth their unique value and create the greatest impact.

- I hired, trained, supervised, and mentored dozens of staff and consultants at Centered Retreat Center, building a unified team that successfully led a website and rebranding strategy.

PROFESSIONAL EXPERIENCE
Director of Operations, Rethink Environment (New York, NY) 2013-present

Member of the senior management team of an internationally recognized environmental organization. Oversee human resources, marketing and communications, information technology, and legal.

A summary sentence allows you to shape your own narrative and helps readers get an immediate sense of your skills and experience. After you've described your primary role and/or accomplishments, you might want to explain the organization's mission if it adds clarity for the reader.

- Build and strengthen internal operations by activating a diverse staff of over 300 people around the globe at staff meetings, regular trainings, and semiannual offsite gatherings.

- In support of a $100M operating budget, collaborate with finance, sales, and registration teams to maximize program revenues.

- Helped develop a strategic plan that revamped the organization's vision and mission.

- Through iterative and collaborative processes, revamped a comprehensive and legally compliant employee handbook through an equity lens to ensure safety and respect in the workplace.

Director of Marketing, Centered Retreat Center (Ithaca, NY) 2008-2013

Led staff and teams at a year-round New York retreat center attended by 20,000 guests annually.

- Worked closely with program staff to develop and oversee marketing and outreach.
- Produced annual program catalog and seasonal mailers distributed to over 30,000 households.
- Managed internal communications and external public relations. Edited grants and program reports.

Traveler, Year Abroad (Vietnam, Cambodia, Brazil, Argentina) 2007–2008

Spent a year traveling visiting farmers' markets around the globe. Grateful for the adventure and the opportunity to explore different people and cultures.

Link to my blog.

Entrepreneurial Chef, Palatable (Boston, MA) 2005–2007

Founded an in-home personal chef service, applying a love of people and food to inspire the palates of omnivores, herbivores, and hungry people of all ages.

- Conducted research and marketing to establish a business plan and client base for over 50 families.
- Managed client relations and services, including menu planning, food selection, and preparation.

Corporate Associate, Evergreen Associates (Boston, MA) 1998–2005

Provided general legal counsel to individual clients, public and private corporations, and nonprofit organizations.

- Analyzed, drafted, and negotiated contracts, employee benefit plans, and legal opinions.
- Researched state and federal tax, bankruptcy, and general corporate laws.
- Designed teaching materials and conducted dozens of training sessions for legal service clinic students, reaching hundreds of people.

VOLUNTEER and COMMUNITY INVOLVEMENT
Contributing Writer, Wash Life Magazine 2008

- Contributed to editorial content for an urban magazine with a circulation of 115,000. Edited articles on topics including environmentalism, food and wine, gardening, and urban design.
- Edited feature interviews with Ina Garten and Annie Leibovitz, among others.

This is an example of how to narrate a gap in employment, especially if you want to highlight a specific skill and the experience you gained.

It's okay to include links to your LinkedIn profile, personal websites, portfolios, and/ or blogs, as long as the content is appropriate. Here, Donna wanted to highlight her writing.

CONTINUING EDUCATION
Certified Nonprofit Accounting, Fiscal Management
Associates, New York, 2019

COMPUTER SKILLS
MS Office Suite, Adobe Creative Suite, Salesforce,
WordPress, Google Drive, Mailchimp, Slack

EDUCATION
Juris Doctor, Drexel University School of Law, 1998
Bachelor of Arts, Colgate University, 1996

Common résumé questions

✔ **Should I have a functional or chronological résumé?** Use a combination of the two. A purely functional résumé, organized by skill set, can be difficult to follow, and a chronological format doesn't allow you to direct your narrative. You'll want a chronological format with your most recent experience first and you can use the bullet points to highlight the skills that you want to demonstrate.

✔ **How much should I customize my résumé?** As we mentioned, you'll want a résumé that you customize slightly, by adding in key words and reordering bullets in your work experience rather than creating a new résumé each time you apply for a job.

✔ **What is the ideal length?** One-page résumés are still fairly common, but typically a 2–3 page résumé is often necessary if you have a few years of work experience. Sectors and industries have different standards for how much you share; for example, jobs in education usually require a complete CV and page count doesn't matter.

✔ **How do I show my impact?** You'll want to use a mix of qualitative and quantitative metrics to paint a vivid picture of your contribution, depending on the nature of your work. Steer away from just listing the responsibilities in your job description. It's often difficult to show impact without 2–3 lines per bullet.

✔ **How do I showcase impact when the organization I've worked for has limited my ability to contribute?** Focus on the role's responsibilities and anything you're proud of. Talk about a process you may have been a part of and what you did to contribute to a project that was important to you.

✔ **Should I leave experiences out that are from more than 15–20 years ago?** It's important to share the totality of your experiences instead of leaving gaps in your résumé. At the same time, do what feels most aligned to you. Trust your gut if it's telling you to leave something out.

✔ **How do I represent my freelancing and/or concurrent work?** Side gigs are relevant experience, and you should include them either as part of your professional experience or as its own section.

✔ **What should I do if I have a gap in my work history?** Address it. For instance, if you were a caregiver or took time to volunteer or travel, include that information in your résumé, if you're comfortable doing so.

✔ **Should I include dates for my education?** If you're farther along in your career, you may prefer to remove specific dates on your résumé, although we typically find that if you remove dates from your education, it tends to indicate to the reader that you're older. Unfortunately, age discrimination still exists, so follow your personal instinct.

✔ **I've taken a lot of online courses and have certifications. How much should I share?** While we encourage you to share what you've learned, you'll want to carefully decide what to include in your résumé, depending on the nature of the role and what skills you're hoping to convey.

Create a One-of-a-Kind Cover Letter

Cover letters, while sometimes anxiety-provoking and difficult to write, are an excellent opportunity to start a dialogue with a hiring manager or organization and explore how you might contribute. This is the virtuous cycle in action! The goal is to authentically connect what you have to offer to what an organization needs, clearly showing how you can add value.

Old Paradigm	New Paradigm
You include a laundry list of your experiences and expertise without providing enough context or details to bring them to life.	You use visual imagery and narrative to illustrate your experience and expertise, conveying how you approach your work and what you've created.
You write things like, "I'm a perfect fit for this position" and try to convince the reader of your value.	You emphasize what draws you to the opportunity and how your unique value can serve the organization. Your letter sets the stage for exploring ways of working together and even sharing ideas, if appropriate.
You focus on yourself and how this role will help you.	You focus on the organization's goals and how your unique value can serve the organization.
You don't mention what draws you to the organization's culture and values.	You highlight your understanding of the organization's culture and values and how they reflect yours (if they do).
You tone down your personality to try to fit into what you think the organization wants.	You use a format and style that reflects your personality and communication style. You might include links to articles you've written and work products, if appropriate.

Kickstart Your Cover Letter

Before sitting down to write your cover letter, spend 20–30 minutes on the following steps so you can really hit the ground running in an intentional way:

- Ask yourself: Why do I really want this particular job? What is specifically drawing me to this organization?
- Review the job description carefully, grouping the responsibilities and qualifications into categories if they aren't already, to better understand the skills required.
- For each responsibility and preferred qualification, quickly brainstorm examples of your relevant skills and experiences, drawing on the work you've done in this book, especially around your unique value and ideal work.
- Brainstorm ideas for what you want to do in the position. *Automatic writing* can be a helpful tool for this. Doing additional research on industry/sector trends can also help you formulate your ideas and get your creative juices flowing.

In these cover letter examples, we've included an abbreviated version of a cover letter Lauren submitted during her job search as well as a modified client example.

EXAMPLE COVER LETTER #1

Dear Dunder Mifflin team:

I'm passionate about empowering managers and helping teams work better so they can thrive in their work and in the world. Seven years of management consulting and another seven in organizational development and coaching provide me with a strong foundation for the leadership and learning role. I bring a broad range of experience supporting leadership development, career development, and talent management. I admire Dunder Mifflin's commitment to developing its talent and building a culture around shaping ideas, a bias for action, and ownership. This ethos meshes well with my penchant for creativity and experimenting with new ideas. I'm excited about the opportunity to contribute to your organizational culture as a member of your staff.

I've created and delivered dozens of adult learning programs and workshops for organizations ranging from a major Jewish nonprofit to a cutting-edge neuroanalytic advertising firm. At the Schusterman Foundation, I envisioned, secured funding for, and co-facilitated *CareerLeap*, a leadership program for mid-career professionals that included a two-day in-person workshop, virtual learning, and coaching. One participant shared: "Through *CareerLeap*, I got a roadmap of practical tools and methodologies for thinking about my job search and career path, an inspirational experience... and most important, an amazing 1:1 coach to help me talk through the most difficult aspects of my job transition." I'm eager to envision and facilitate trainings and workshops at Dunder Mifflin using a variety of learning techniques and modalities.

I believe a coaching mindset is an essential tool for managers, and it's a way to support creative problem-solving to build strong teams. I have coached hundreds of individuals since becoming a certified coach, and I tap into this knowledge when meeting with individual contributors, managers, and executives to help them navigate difficult conversations and complicated staffing issues. The coaching approaches I have learned have also given me the confidence to deal with conflict and team dynamics in the moment. Recently, for example, I did an

Use your opening paragraph to describe what specifically is drawing you to the position and the organization, along with a sneak preview of your unique value and mission.

If relevant, include links to your articles and/ or portfolio. Lauren hyperlinked to some of the projects she's completed, not shown in this example.

Make the link to the full range of the organization's needs. That not only includes the position's responsibilities but also specific skills and qualifications. Lauren shares her approach to coaching, which directly relates to the responsibilities in the job description.

intervention to diffuse a heated interaction between two leaders who were arguing about a missed grant deadline, and who were avoiding the underlying dynamics beneath the surface.

My work as a consultant has honed my ability to help organizations quickly identify areas of need and find potential solutions. For the World Association of Girl Guides and Girl Scouts, I conducted a three-month review of four global leadership centers, assessing HR, operations, finance, and programs. At Marcum, I oversee project teams to ensure that we're putting forward high-quality deliverables within a tight timeline, while also ensuring that our clients are informed and up-to-date about our process.

Primarily focus on sharing examples from your current job and also some from previous roles, if relevant.

I am highly collaborative, and I enjoy creating space for employees to share their ideas so they feel heard as we partner on projects and work toward a shared goal.

I look forward to further discussing this role and how I might be able to contribute to Dunder Mifflin. Thank you for considering me.

Keep the closing paragraph short and to the point. If you have attached other supplemental documents or references (besides a résumé), please note that here.

Best,
Lauren Weinstein

EXAMPLE COVER LETTER #2

March 1, 2021

Dear Executive Leadership Team,

I am excited to apply for the Chief Program Officer position to manage a diverse team, drive innovation, and forge new partnerships at Humanitarian International. Your work is profoundly important, and I have been moved by the organization's commitment to welcoming refugees. I am eager to bring my skills and insights to Humanitarian International to help address what I see as one of the biggest challenges of our time. I have been involved in community-based organizations for the last 15 years and seek to work on a more national and global scale. Note that I'm based in Austin but would absolutely consider moving to New York for the position.

Convening People and Facilitating Meaningful Experiences

In my current role, I build deep trust with a range of stakeholders across the public and private sectors. When the pandemic began, I organized a community-wide leadership call right before shelter-in-place took effect. In doing so, I created a space for nonprofit leaders to share concerns and contingency plans for their organizations. Because I received so much positive feedback about the openness and wisdom shared on that call, I have continued to host and curate ongoing gatherings. This has allowed local leaders to continuously learn from each other and dialogue with government officials to make strategic decisions as the pandemic unfolded.

Most recently, I facilitated a process for board members to rethink my organization's three-year funding priorities. Over six committee meetings, I managed multiple viewpoints, helping to clarify ideas until there was consensus that reflected our shared thinking. In addition to my facilitation skills, I bring a sense of calm to a room that is useful during tense moments. At Humanitarian International, I'd love to bring my skills as a facilitator to bridge the gaps between different stakeholders to make sure that we create vibrant programs addressing refugees' needs.

Date your letter and address it to the hiring manager or person listed on the job description. You can also address it to a specific team or the organization, like Sasha does.

Indicate your willingness to relocate if the job is located in a specified place, only if you're really open to moving.

You'll want to write approximately 3–5 paragraphs highlighting your unique value, your impact, and your ideas. You may consider organizing the sections by key headers you identified when you reviewed the job description.

Managing a Team and Building Team Dynamics

As a manager, I operate on a "no surprises" model—I share what I can about what's happening at various levels of the organization and invite my team's input whenever possible. One of my catch phrases is "I am brainstorming here, jump in!" I use it to signal that I am sharing my own process and that there is room for my team to both influence my decision-making and to safely try out their own ideas.

In supervision sessions, I expect those on my team to discern which details I need to know and when to seek my input. I also remove obstacles when I can and help my team build their own capacity in finding workarounds. It is my practice to offer a lot of feedback immediately and without any drama. As a result, I build trust across the team and foster an environment of self-reflection and personal development—which I think would help Humanitarian International staff feel valued and supported in their day-to-day work.

Creating Partnerships and Increasing Innovation

I very much enjoy the creative process of dreaming up new ideas. I was trained in social entrepreneurship and previously ran a small matchmaking company. In my current role, I often develop pilot programs quickly and inexpensively. Then, using the data I glean from the pilots, I am able to present the board and funders the information that we need to evaluate whether to invest. One such program I ran focused on engaging Baby Boomers in political giving that eventually involved hundreds of local community members each month. This is just one example of how I have launched projects, gathered feedback, refined strategy, and grown a program. I would like to use this approach at Humanitarian International to strengthen the power of your network while developing fruitful new partnerships.

I deeply believe in your programming, as you build structured support for refugees and relationships with local community members. I would love to discuss ideas to build a plan for an alumni network and also see opportunities to bring more awareness about the current state of immigration.

I look forward to the possibility of speaking with you about the role of Chief Program Officer and learning more about your needs and goals.

Thank you for your consideration!
Sasha

Use action verbs and do your best to paint a picture of how you've effected change or describe what you've created in your past or current roles.

Throughout your letter, show that you've done your research on the position and organization, using language that is common in the industry or from the job description if it's authentic to you.

Common Cover Letter Questions

✔ **Do I really need to put together a cover letter, even when it's not requested?** Yes, unless you're already connected with the hiring manager through an introduction and they have directly told you not to. The letter exponentially increases your ability to influence how the hiring manager perceives your fit with the position, providing details that reinforce and expand on your résumé.

✔ **How long should my cover letter be?** Stick to two pages max and shorter if that's the industry standard. Usually, it's not possible to write a really good and descriptive cover letter in less than three-quarters of a page.

✔ **Do I need to address all the responsibilities and qualifications in the job description?** We recommend that you review the job description very carefully to understand exactly what the organization is looking for and make sure to cover all of the desired skills and experiences.

✔ **How is my cover letter different if I'm responding to specific questions or prompts in the job description?** You'll want to respond thoroughly to all of the questions. You may choose to add additional information that illuminates your unique value and accomplishments if it feels useful to share.

✔ **Should I discuss missing skills or gaps in my experience?** Yes! Address any gap directly. You should explain what transferable skills you have, using sector-specific language, as well as how you're building related skills. Also, if you're switching sectors or job functions, share additional information early on in your cover letter to help the reader understand your career trajectory.

✔ **Do I need to acknowledge any gaps in employment?** If you've addressed these gaps in your résumé, you don't need to expand on them in your cover letter. If there are skills you've gained during a gap in employment, you may want to share if they're relevant to the job description.

✔ **Will sharing additional or supplemental materials help my application?** It depends. If you have something that you think would deepen the reader's understanding of your unique value, such as a case study or printed brochure, share it. You can include it or mention it at the end of your cover letter.

WHEN TO BRING IN INSIDER INFORMATION OR HAVE SOMEONE PUT IN A GOOD WORD FOR YOU

A lot of our clients ask us when they should reach out to someone they know in an organization to learn more about a role or "put in a good word." Typically, an opportune moment is when you're applying or early in the interviewing process—so you can learn more about the role and the organization and ask any questions that you might have. Doing this might also help bring more visibility to your application, and if you haven't applied yet, help you get an interview.

If you're looking for someone to put in a good word for you, tread carefully. It's important to consider how that person is perceived within the organization. Sometimes asking someone to "endorse" you while you're actively interviewing can backfire. It really depends on the interviewer and organizational culture. In addition, be careful about how many individuals you reach out to who work at the organization where you're interviewing, who aren't actively part of the interview process. Contacting multiple people in an organization during the hiring process can be risky since you could be perceived as someone who oversteps boundaries. Do what feels right to you given the organizational dynamics you've observed and your own communication style.

Choose Your References Wisely

Be ready to provide contact information for at least three individuals who can speak to your skills, experience, working style, and unique value, as well as why a particular position is a good fit for you. We recommend that one reference be a previous manager, preferably your most recent one, if possible. You'll also want another reference from someone you've supervised (if you have that experience) and a professional recommendation such as a colleague, a board member, or community partner.

When you're thinking about selecting references, consider the following:

- They know you and your unique value, like you as a person, and want to see you do well.
- You have an idea about what they might say and you think the reference will be positive even if they highlight some of the areas where you might be able to grow or improve.
- They are open to having a conversation with you about the job you're applying for, if you ask.

Do your best to discern if your references will provide enough detail and help your future employer understand your unique value. Some people who may be a big fan of yours might not be good at articulating specific examples of your successes. If you're not sure, perhaps test out the waters by asking for a LinkedIn reference first. It's ideal to reach out to potential references before you start applying for jobs and share more context. It's also a great way to reconnect with people in your community.

Many of our clients are concerned about sharing references from their current job, especially if they don't feel comfortable with their team or manager knowing they're looking for something new. We've found that employers are often sensitive to requests not to reach out to current colleagues, and are able to find references that work for them and the employer. If for some reason a potential employer is not sensitive to this request, that's likely a red flag.

Who do you think could be references for you, given the criteria above?

_____

_____

_____

When it's time to share reference information with a potential employer, be sure to include the reference's name, title, and organization, contact information (phone and email), and how the reference knows you (i.e., in what capacity and for how long). And avoid writing "references available upon request" on any of your material.

Write Your Own Work Proposal

One of Cathy's clients has ideas around how to bring people together in creative ways. Before COVID, he created in-person events and gatherings to bring people together. When he was laid off, he started to have a few informal conversations about this passion. In a conversation with a former colleague, he shared some of these ideas, and the response he got was super positive, even though he didn't have a clear partner in mind. With that encouragement and the desire to really tap into his unique value, he wrote a work proposal and shared his ideas with a few organizations. Ultimately, he found a partner who shared a similar vision.

If you have a specific role that you've imagined for yourself but you're not seeing it, or an idea that you're excited about, you might want to write a work proposal. Work proposals can take many forms—an email, a two-to-four-page memo, or a visual presentation complete with graphs and charts.

What to include in your work proposal:

- Explain how your idea, whether it's a project, program, or position potentially could help solve a gap for the organization or the industry/sector.

- Elaborate on your specific idea, approach, or innovation and show supporting data, if you can. You'll want to make a business case for what will be improved or changed as a result of what you're proposing, along with your role.

- Try to anticipate questions. If you are proposing a specific project or service, think through whether it makes sense to include a timeline, staffing needs, processes, structures, pricing, and more.

Most successful work proposals build on existing relationships, but don't let that stop you if you have a strong idea and deep expertise. Start with a brief email or a one-page overview to gauge interest before sending a more detailed proposal.

Example Work Proposal

Below is an example work proposal that Lauren wrote to the CEO of a company she was considering joining a few years ago. She wrote this note after she met with the CEO and had additional conversations with other senior leaders. The CEO was eager to not only improve internal talent management but also build out a new business offering that Lauren would lead.

Lauren had some hesitations about the role the CEO initially proposed after she met with senior leaders who were not on board with the new business offering. She decided to share some of her observations with the CEO and also detail a few possibilities for roles if she joined the company.

EXAMPLE WORK PROPOSAL

Dear John,

I enjoyed our conversation about potential opportunities at Initech. I want to share thoughts and open questions I have about the role you're envisioning for me:

- I think that the technology platform you're considering can be added into your existing offerings for clients. Based on my experience in the industry and what I heard from your team, however, I don't think your clients are likely to purchase this offering given their small budget for this type of software and their perceived value of the product.

- I wonder about the long-term sustainability of implementing this technology platform. How do you set up the offering/subscription service so that clients can access the product without relying on the software provider to continuously use it? What type of support would your company need to provide to clients?

Below are some ideas about different roles I could play at Initech:

- Join the client-facing consulting team that focuses on strategy and leadership.
- Serve the organization in an internal capacity as a Talent Advisor or provide structure to the overall team of Talent Advisors.
- Develop a new business line of leadership development offerings for clients.

I'm very interested in continuing the conversation and exploring what might be most helpful for Initech.

Thanks so much,
Lauren

We recommend highlighting your understanding of the role and, if relevant, internal dynamics or trends in the marketplace.

In this example, Lauren highlights a few concrete ideas, focusing on joining a team or building out new offerings. If you are proposing a completely new role or program, provide as much detail as possible.

Reiterate your interest and next steps, if possible.

How to Deal with Your Emotions if You Don't Hear Back

Applying for jobs can be emotionally charged, to say the least! The application process is difficult and time-consuming. On top of it, waiting to hear back can be frustrating and it's not in your control. And let's be real; it's crappy when people don't get back to you—an all-too-common occurrence. So what do you do?

It's normal to want to hear back as soon as possible, and it's difficult to be in limbo. As we mentioned earlier in this chapter, it can sometimes take several weeks to hear back on an application, so don't despair (yet)! Not hearing back doesn't necessarily mean you're not being considered—it might reflect the pace of the organization's hiring process or possibly that they are reconsidering the details of the role.

As you think about how to best follow up, consider what is motivating you. For example, are you trying to relieve some of your anxiety? Now is a great time to turn to the Emotional Breakthrough Process and work through difficult emotions such as anxiety. When you do this, you actively build your resilience, sense of self, and power.

Another way to activate your power is to follow up in a way that reflects your authentic interest in the role, where you are in the process, and how much time has passed.

The real opportunity is to dig deep and recognize your worth, even if you don't feel validated or respected by the process itself.

If you're wondering when to follow up, let any instructions in the application be your guide. If the organization requests no calls or emails, respect that. At any point, you may choose to reach out to individuals who might have insider information about the position to learn more, but as we mentioned earlier, be cautious about overstepping boundaries in the hiring process.

WHEN TO FOLLOW UP ON AN APPLICATION AND/OR INTERVIEW

You've submitted an application	After 2 weeks, send a follow-up email. You can then follow up about a month later if you still haven't heard back to ask what the timeline is and next steps.
You've had at least one interview	If you haven't heard back 2–3 weeks after your first interview, it's appropriate to follow up and ask if there's any update on the job and next steps.
You're in the final stages of interviewing	Follow up every 2 weeks or so to check in and ask for an update. If you haven't heard back after you've reached out a few times, unfortunately, it's likely you're not moving forward at this point.

Celebrate **AND MAINTAIN MOMENTUM**

Now is a moment to celebrate your very intense work in this chapter and also take stock of what you're learning about yourself and the job search. Even writing about applying to jobs is stressful; we definitely took time to celebrate after completing this chapter! Be patient and kind to yourself as you apply to jobs and wait to hear back. Follow up on your applications and with your community to share updates and find sources of inspiration and hope.

Chapter 8

GET READY FOR THE INTERVIEW PROCESS

Get into a PREPARED mindset

Start preparing for interviews

Bite-size your interview prep

Navigate the interview

How to follow up on an interview

What to do when you're "rejected"

Take a step back and recalibrate

Celebrate and maintain momentum

Rachel, a twenty-seven-year-old human resources manager, was struggling with a difficult manager she didn't trust. And she was tired of working in a rigid, hierarchical organization—she felt stifled by the bureaucracy. She decided to start looking for a new HR position with the goal of working at a smaller company with a less traditional organizational structure.

Outgoing and a self-described extrovert, Rachel generally enjoys meeting new people and considers herself comfortable speaking in public and being interviewed. But as she navigated the job search process during COVID, she felt uncharacteristically uncomfortable during Zoom interviews.

Working with Cathy, Rachel analyzed what was going on. For one, she felt awkward discussing her current work situation and the dynamic with her manager. Additionally, the interviews had multiple participants, and it was difficult to read the audience over Zoom. Rachel found herself getting frustrated and speaking for too long as she shared examples of the work she had done.

Through coaching with Cathy, Rachel practiced her talking points and created an "inner psyche prompt" to center and connect to herself during interviews. Rachel focused on what she could control: what she shared and how she shared it. She developed short sound bites that conveyed her unique value and articulated her clarity around organizational culture and the importance of having a flexible, non-hierarchical work environment. This helped her get a great new job leading HR for a smaller company, that felt her approach to organizational culture really meshed with theirs.

Finding out that you have an interview, especially after a lot of hard work, can be both exciting and anxiety provoking! It can make us feel like we have to sell ourselves. In the new work paradigm, we see the interview process as another opportunity to enter the virtuous cycle even though we recognize that many organizations continue to set up the process as if they're solely determining fit.

Still, interviews are an incredible opportunity for you and your potential employer to discern if you're a mutual fit and explore whether your potential colleagues are people who you're eager to work with. Even though an unequal power is often at play, we hope that by doing the work in this chapter, you feel more empowered to discern for yourself whether a job works for you as you interview. In this chapter, we break down the interview process so you are better prepared and know how to follow up.

Get into a **<u>PREPARED</u>** Mindset

Being prepared starts by getting centered with your morning practice the day of your interview. One of Cathy's clients does a specific three-mile run near her home before job interviews. Lauren likes to get mentally ready for interviews the way she used to warm up for races when she was a college swimmer: carb-load the night before and use visualization techniques.

Additionally, as you prepare for an interview, check back in with your feelings and needs. If you're really interested in a job, even if you've done a lot of preparation, it's totally normal to experience strong emotion. Use the Emotional Breakthrough Process to tap into your sense of confidence.

Try developing an inner psyche prompt like Rachel did—a phrase or keyword that you say inside your head to help you stay connected to your unique value in case you get tripped up in the interview. For example, *"I'm really proud of my ability to brainstorm new solutions"* or *"Take a deep breath."* By having prompts at the ready, you'll be better able to respond from a place of empowerment.

What could you develop as your inner psyche prompts? Jot down a few ideas.

_____

_____

_____

You'll also want to pay attention to the way you dress, making sure it reflects your authentic style while being mindful of the organization's vibe. Many of our clients report that the way they dress for interviews helps them feel more confident and prepared.

Start Preparing for Interviews

Every interview process is different, depending on the organization, interviewer(s), and the norms in the industry/sector. For example, some interview processes move fairly quickly and involve two to three rounds, while others can take several months with numerous people involved.

First-round interviews and subsequent interviews vary drastically from one organization to the next. Some organizations ask you to respond to a scenario or complete some type of assignment. For instance, if you're interviewing to be an executive director, you might be asked to prepare a presentation on how you would bolster fundraising and develop a strategic plan. If you're a finalist for a marketing position, you may be given twenty-four hours to write a series of tweets on a particular topic.

Because it's difficult to predict exactly what will be included in an interview process, it's important to prepare as much as possible—and that takes time.

As you prepare, pay attention to your feelings and whether you would really be interested in doing the job. That can be quite empowering as you discern fit.

NAVIGATE A SCREENING CALL WITH A RECRUITER OR PRERECORDED VIDEO INTERVIEW

Depending on the norms of your industry, you might have an initial screening conversation about a job with an internal HR person or external recruiter. These are typically 15–20 minute conversations where you'll likely be asked a few questions about prior experience, when you're available to start, as well as your salary range. But you could be asked almost any interview question, so it's best if you do most of your interview prep beforehand.

You may even be asked to do a prerecorded video interview before speaking with a real human being. If this is the case, you'll want to be mindful of how you craft your response within the allotted time period. Try to imagine that you're having a conversation with someone and practice a few times before you decide what to share.

Bite-Size Your Interview Prep

You've overhauled your résumé, had myriad conversations with individuals in your network, and perfected your cover letter! And all of that work has paid off. Bite-sizing your interview prep, like so many other parts of the job search, will make it more manageable.

SAMPLE BITE-SIZE TASKS

✔ Read relevant blogs, articles, and thought pieces for additional perspectives on the job function, organization, and industry.

✔ Look at the job description and come up with questions that you think you'll be asked and practice your answers.

✔ Develop a set of talking points and examples for each question you expect to be asked. Make sure that you're prepared to share examples of previous work experiences that directly relate to the responsibilities listed in a job description. These examples should be no more than two minutes long and provide brief context, a description of your role, and the outcome.

✔ Brainstorm potential ideas you have about the position (which you've likely done already in your cover letter).

✔ Prepare at least two to five questions you have about the organization and position, so you can discern whether the position, the organization, and culture are a good fit for you.

✔ Practice interviewing with a friend, colleague, or coach. Consider recording yourself on video and reviewing it to refine your talking points and examples.

✔ Look up the interviewers on LinkedIn to learn about their experience. (But be cautious about directly sharing what you may have learned—you could come across as a private detective.)

Navigate the Interview

While some people love interviewing, for many it can feel awkward. Some of our clients have told us that they've felt like they're performing on a stage, with the attendant stage fright that feeling can provoke. Virtual interviews over Zoom only exacerbate that feeling, making it difficult to read body language and reactions, as Rachel experienced.

Throughout the interview, make sure that you're answering questions directly and tying in specific examples that you prepared. If you're given a tough question or one that you don't have an immediate answer for, reflect quickly before responding. You might say, *"Good question"* or *"Let me think about that for a moment."* You can also briefly glance at your cover letter or résumé to get ideas of what to share.

You'll want to show personality without overdoing it or getting off topic. Be responsive to the interviewer's energy and style without losing yourself in it. Being in both a prepared and present mindset will help you attend to your physical and emotional reaction during your interview with more ease.

Try to pay attention to your thoughts and feelings while being present in the conversation. Notice what your body language might convey through your eye contact, facial expressions, tone and volume of your voice, and posture.

If you don't know how to respond, you can say, *"It's not something I've thought about in-depth. Let me take a moment to reflect on it."* You can also ask to come back to the question at the end of the interview or in a follow-up note. If you aren't clear on the question, don't be afraid to ask for clarification.

COMMON INTERVIEW QUESTIONS

Question	How to Respond	What to Avoid
Tell me about yourself and your background. Why are you interested in this position? Why now?	Connect the dots between your unique value and the organization's needs and why your skills and experiences are a good fit for this specific role.	Don't share a laundry list of everything you've done or your entire work trajectory. Avoid rambling and telling disjointed stories.
What are your strengths?	Give direct and very specific answers that showcase how you've made a difference in your work and link your response directly to what the organization needs.	Try not to convince the interviewer of your strengths, coming across like you're trying to persuade them of your value or that you're desperate for the position.
What are your weaknesses / blind spots?	Answer directly and talk about your self-awareness. Share a specific example of how you've observed yourself and your ability to course correct.	Avoid hiding your vulnerabilities or turning them into strengths. And definitely don't give a generic response like, "I'm a perfectionist."

Question	How to Respond	What to Avoid
Can you give me an example of an accomplishment related to...(a specific skill and/ or a particular experience)?	Set the context and help the interviewer understand how the example you're sharing is relevant. Talk through the key steps you took and how it impacted the people involved. Share what you've learned and possibly what you would do differently going forward.	Share a generic response that doesn't describe the depth and breadth of your work.
Which of the responsibilities is most/least interesting to you?	This is another opportunity to share a specific example of what you've created in the past and how it relates to the job description. Perhaps share a potential idea.	You're unprepared and stumble over the question. You say that everything is equally interesting to you and don't offer a thoughtful analysis of how you perceive the role.
Can you share an example of when you had to deal with a conflict at work?	Showcase your self-awareness and how you problem-solve and bring creativity to difficult situations.	Blame the other person or avoid sharing what your responsibility in the conflict may have been.
Tell me about your management and leadership style.	Share a vivid example of how you specifically activate people and rally them around a larger vision.	Talk about how you like to lead teams without providing an explanation or example.
What type of work environment and culture do you thrive in?	Articulate aspects of your ideal work, pointing to organizational culture and mission, as well as team dynamics.	Talk about bad work environments or a terrible manager you had.

HOW TO TALK ABOUT BEING LAID OFF

If you are asked why you left a specific job or were laid off, tell the truth without oversharing. You certainly don't want to badmouth your company, manager, or team. Depending on the circumstance, you may need to walk the fine line between explaining your situation and going into too many details, which could come across as defensive. For example, if you parted ways with your previous organization because you didn't get along with the board chair, you might diplomatically respond, *"My board and I didn't agree on the strategic vision and funding model for the organization."*

You may also decide to briefly share what you've learned from the experience in a matter-of-fact way, showing your self-awareness and growth. *"The organization had three major funders and one withdrew their support, so the leadership decided it could no longer support our program. I've learned that it's risky to rely too heavily on one funder."* Practice your response so you get comfortable with how you describe what happened and remember to keep it short. We're finding that there's more empathy and less stigma to being let go or furloughed, especially in unpredictable times.

How to Follow Up on an Interview

Take the time to process your immediate thoughts and feelings after the interview. Write down what you think went well, what responses you might tweak in the future, and what additional questions or concerns you still have about the position. And celebrate your progress! Treat yourself to a scoop of ice cream or call up a friend to tell them about the interview.

You'll also want to write a thank you email. However, if it feels appropriate, you might want to send a handwritten note, for example, if you're applying for a job that requires fundraising or client relationship building. During her most recent job search, Lauren had seven interviews with six people, and she sent each a customized thank you email to share gratitude and reiterate key points about the role and the organization.

EXAMPLE THANK YOU NOTE

Below is a thank you note that Lauren wrote to a group of people she interviewed with in one of her job searches.

Dear _____,

Thanks for meeting me yesterday. I have enjoyed getting to know you a bit, and I'm excited about the opportunity to work at Initech. The work itself—partnering with clients on leadership and organizational challenges and providing coaching to the company's employees—is an incredible opportunity that I'm eager to partner on.

I want to briefly emphasize a few areas where I can add value:

> A thank you note is a great way to reiterate your unique value.

First, since a central part of this job will be working with senior leaders, I want to underscore my experience in this area. In my current job, I advise more than thirty senior leaders at nonprofits across the country. As a talent advisor and coach to them, I discuss hiring practices and provide feedback on job descriptions as well as recruiting strategies.

Secondly, I know this job will require a self-starter who can sell and deliver projects. I pride myself on maintaining strong client relationships and have shown that I can drum up new business opportunities and deliver on the work. While I was an independent consultant, for example, I built a relationship with a leader at Columbia Business School and was subsequently hired to oversee a project for them.

> While Lauren didn't share any specific articles or resources, you may decide to if there's an organic way to follow-up on something you discussed in the interview.

Lastly, I've shown I can work within a framework, but also outside of it when needed. My Accenture background has provided me with processes and tools that I can utilize as a consultant. Meanwhile, my work as both an independent consultant and my current role have enabled me to develop creative approaches in the moment with limited supervision.

> It's important to follow up and address any concerns that might have come up in the interview process. Here, Lauren felt the need to share additional information about her skills and experience because she sensed that the interviewers had lingering questions.

I look forward to continuing the conversation and discussing next steps!

Thanks again, Lauren

Even if you're no longer interested in a position, we recommend following up and thanking the interviewers and briefly letting them know why.

For example, you might write,

> "Thank you so much again for taking the time to interview me. I've thought more deeply about the role, and while I have great respect for your mission, I realize that the position requires more focus on product marketing than product development. At this point in my career, I'm really interested in being hands-on in developing new products. I would definitely like to stay in touch and am interested if other opportunities focused on product development emerge."

If you interviewed with a group, it's okay to write one note to everyone you met, unless you feel that you have enough to write to each person individually. And if you're working with a recruiter, it's equally important to write a note of gratitude—this small act can have ripple effects down the road.

What to Do When You're "Rejected"

That email you've been dreading lands like a grenade in your inbox. *"We really enjoyed meeting you, however we're moving forward with another candidate."* Or, *"It was great to meet you, and I hope we have opportunities to collaborate in the future."* Even worse, you receive a form email sent by a robot suggesting you *"Check our website at jobs.insensitive.com for future opportunities."*

Ugh. We really feel for you. Looking for a new job is so personal and can feel very vulnerable. You've invested a lot of time and emotional energy in the process. So when you don't hear back, or you make it to the final rounds of an interview process and aren't given an offer, it can really hurt. Especially when it happens repeatedly. It feels like rejection.

You have a right to feel *whatever* you're feeling. You might want to take time to sit and reflect on the process. Moments like these, as difficult as they can be, are opportunities to practice connecting to yourself and looking at what's in and out of your control. We recommend working with the Emotional Breakthrough Process once again. When you face feelings of inadequacy, sadness, and disappointment, take time to sort through what your needs are.

When they don't get a job offer, some of our clients take time for reflection and solitude; others get inspired to create an action plan. If, for example, one of your needs is to feel validated, work on a professional development plan or ask a friend, trusted mentor, or coach to connect and give you positive reinforcement.

If you've had at least one interview, consider asking for feedback from the hiring manager, people you've interviewed with, or a recruiter you've worked with. Sometimes reaching out to someone that you connected with can be a good place to start. Ask for general feedback and, if appropriate, what skills or experiences they felt you lacked. You might even want to ask for advice, especially if you're looking for similar types of roles in the same industry.

Stay open to the feedback and come back to the *front door formula* on page 118. You need to discern what feedback, if any, you want to let in. For example, if an organization you interviewed with gives you feedback that they were worried that you wouldn't be able to meet their ambitious sales targets, how will you let that affect you? How can you learn and grow from it?

Take a Step Back and Recalibrate

Sometimes, at this point, it's helpful to step back and reflect on your application and interviewing experience to-date, especially if you aren't making the progress you want.

Ask yourself and your support team:

- Is there something about the way I'm interviewing that's not conveying my unique value and what I'm capable of?
- Am I applying for jobs that I'm overqualified for or, on the other hand, are too much of a stretch given my skills and experiences?
- Are the jobs that I'm applying for aligned with my ideal job, must-haves, and deal breakers?
- Am I conveying my unique value in my application materials and follow-up communications?

Given your responses, how might you shift your approach to applying for jobs? Do you need to pivot in any way? Depending on how things are going, you may want to take a short break from the job search to reorient and reenergize. But don't give up!

You need to be your biggest advocate—remind yourself of what's really important to you and what you truly want.

Sometimes it takes a while for things to click, and while a few bad interviewing experiences can be discouraging, stay connected to your feelings and needs.

Celebrate AND MAINTAIN MOMENTUM

We're hopeful that you've made it through a few successful interviews by this point! If you have, be sure to celebrate and do something nice for yourself. Consider what you've learned and how your thinking has shifted about potential jobs. And regardless of where you find yourself, take pride in all the work you've done so far.

Chapter 9

MAKE A DECISION AND NEGOTIATE YOUR OFFER

Get into a GROUNDED mindset

A quick guide to decision-making

Gauge your emotional reaction

Analyze your decision

Tap into your intuition

Make your decision

Prepare to negotiate

Negotiate effectively

Celebrate and maintain momentum

Terrance thought his job interviews with a major university were going great. You're amazing, one interviewer told him. Another said he would be a natural for the academic advisor position he had applied for. But when he got the offer, he was disappointed. The pay was enough to live on, but considerably less than what he thought he deserved. When he let the hiring manager know that he needed a higher salary, he was told that due to hiring rules at the university there was no negotiating.

It was a gut punch. He was excited about the position, but he was frustrated that the bureaucracy of the university placed artificial limits on how much someone could make in a particular role. In a phone conversation with the hiring manager, Terrance had no choice but to say that he couldn't take the offer. In fact, he needed $10,000 more to say yes to the job.

The hiring manager said he would look into it and get back to Terrance. In the conversation, Terrance shared his strategic ideas for the job and decided to point out connections he had that could lead to new fundraising opportunities. He essentially made the business case for hiring himself. "I know it's a huge leap and that there's a formal salary structure in place, but I would be so grateful if you would be willing to consider increasing the salary." He was genuine and even a bit vulnerable, adding, "I'm really excited about this partnership. I hope that we can make it work."

A few days later, Terrance got a call from the hiring manager, offering him 20 percent more than the original offer. The hiring manager recognized the possibilities with Terrance and behind the scenes had lobbied to bring him on at a higher salary. Terrance took the job and stayed there for five years, happy to call the university his second home. And the school recouped its investment many times over as his fundraising skills were indeed a big asset.

You've done it! You got a job offer!

It's an exhilarating moment—and a terrifying one.

While no one can ever know for sure whether a job is the right choice, by this point hopefully you have a good sense of whether or not it is a good fit. Still, there's always a part of making a big decision that requires a leap of faith. Taking that leap of faith is easier when you tap into your feelings and needs. And while there is always a chance that things won't work out exactly as you hoped, if you've taken all the steps outlined in the book, know that you're doing your best!

In this chapter, we lay out how you can make the best decision for yourself. We'll walk you through how to logically analyze your decision, while also staying connected to your feelings, needs, and intuition. Then we'll turn to how to navigate the complexity of negotiation, the ultimate opportunity to step into your power and demonstrate honesty, openness, and the capacity to take responsibility for what you need.

Get into a <u>GROUNDED</u> Mindset

Accepting a new job can feel risky—you're taking an important step in your career and life, and possibly putting other opportunities aside. Your next job will affect your and your family's day-to-day life, happiness, economic well-being, and short-term and long-term goals. It's easier to make a decision when you're grounded and feel a sense of calm and self-connection. Be on the lookout for any emotional hijacks that arise—they're totally normal at this stage because this type of decision can feel like very high stakes.

At the end of your morning practice, remind yourself that you've come this far. Visualize yourself being in a state of calm as you get ready to make a decision. Try to slow down and take some deep breaths. Write down or say to yourself, *"I'm ready to make a great decision for myself and/or me and my family."* Notice your excitement or concern. If you find yourself getting anxious, turn to your support team.

Spend a few minutes and take deep breaths: breathe in for three seconds and exhale for six seconds. Then write down what you notice about yourself and how you feel different, if at all.

HOW TO RESPOND TO AN OFFER IN THE MOMENT

When you do receive an offer, express your gratitude authentically in the moment. This could be as simple as communicating, *"Thank you for the opportunity. I'm excited by the position. I would like to take the next few days to think it through. Can I follow up with any questions that I have on Wednesday?"* You can also ask who you should be in touch with if you have any questions, whether it's HR, your direct potential manager, or someone else. Additionally, you'll want to ask for an offer letter in writing, if you aren't given one.

A Quick Guide to Decision-Making

It can be tempting to immediately say yes when you receive an offer. You might feel internal pressure to respond quickly. You may also feel pressured by your employer and other people in your life. We suggest taking at least twenty-four to forty-eight hours to make your decision, and even up to a week if you need it.

You'll want to feel fully comfortable and address all of your questions and concerns before accepting an offer, which takes time and self-reflection. Make sure to clarify with the hiring manager or recruiter when they need a response back from you.

This is a crucial part of deepening the virtuous cycle, even if you decide not to take the job!

Throughout your life, perhaps without even realizing it, you've been honing your professional career decision-making muscles, so you probably have a good foundation to build upon. You make the best decisions when you access your inner wisdom. We define inner wisdom as the totality of your emotional, rational, and intuitive sides. Sometimes, you might prefer to lead with your emotions and would rather not focus on the rational or intuitive. Other times, you might think it's best to rely on the data you collect rather than your emotions or intuition.

ACCESS YOUR INNER WISDOM TO MAKE BETTER DECISIONS

EMOTIONAL REACTION

RATIONAL ANALYSIS

INTUITION

INNER WISDOM

When you're tapped into your inner wisdom, you'll be more connected to yourself, your community, and the world, and have the necessary data to make the best decision.

Gauge Your Emotional Reaction

Checking in with your feelings, needs, and beliefs can reveal what you really think about a job offer—it's an incredibly powerful lever to make the best decision you can. Values underpin your emotional reality and form the bedrock of decision-making. Checking in with them can be very grounding to tease out why a job is or isn't aligned for you.

Check In with Your Values

Revisit your values in chapter 4 and sit with them as you think about the decision you're making. Some of the values that you hold near and dear may actually be in conflict with each other, complicating your decision-making. *Creative autonomy,* for example, may be important to you, but you may have to compromise in order to take a full-time job that provides *stability,* another important value. If, for instance, you say one of your top values is family, but you're about to accept a job that's 65 hours a week, that may mean that family is an aspirational value and *ambition* is what's really guiding you.

To what degree do you think you can live your values in this job?
Example: Creative autonomy—most definitely, stability—not sure, and family—yes!

Tap into Your Feelings, Needs, and Beliefs Using the Emotional Breakthrough Process

What, if any, limiting or empowering beliefs might be affecting you as you make this decision?

LIMITING BELIEFS	EMPOWERING BELIEFS
Example: This job has a lot of responsibility and maybe there's someone better for it.	*Example: I'm so ready for this opportunity and I'm well prepared for this role.*

As you imagine yourself in the position, ask yourself what are you feeling when you think about accepting the offer?

POSITIVE EMOTIONS:
Example: Happy, excited, and anticipatory

NEGATIVE EMOTIONS:
Example: Nervous and apprehensive

Alternatively, what are you feeling when you think about *not* accepting the offer?

POSITIVE EMOTIONS:
Example: None

NEGATIVE EMOTIONS:
Example: Disappointed, agitated, and sad

If you say *yes* to the position, what needs are met or unmet for you?

MET NEEDS
Example: Stability, inspiration, and dignity.

UNMET NEEDS
Example: Money, recognition, and rest.

If you say *no* to the position, what needs are met or unmet for you?

MET NEEDS
Example: Freedom, independence, and self-expression

UNMET NEEDS
Example: Stability, money, and community

_____

_____

_____

_____

 **Sit with all of the information you've gathered. Which decision feels most aligned for you at this point in the process?**

_____

_____

Whatever your initial decision is, we strongly recommend that you try on saying yes for a few days and then, alternately, saying no for a few days. This will help you further discern the best decision for you.

One of Cathy's clients, a product designer, struggled with whether to accept a job offer. There were a few components that felt off, including salary, the specific job function, and the commute. And yet she was strongly considering saying yes because she loved the dynamics of the team, the vibe at the company, and the possibility of learning from expert colleagues. When she examined her feelings and needs, she felt anxious and realized that her most important unmet need was having a job in the middle of COVID. She turned to her best friend and weighed her options. With more clarity, she decided to accept the offer, knowing that the position provided the stability she desired, and she was willing to live with other aspects that weren't exactly aligned.

Analyze Your Decision

While you may already have some clarity about what decision *feels* right, another important part of accessing your inner wisdom is to take an analytical approach by revisiting your must-haves and deal breakers from chapter 5. Doing so will help you gauge whether the offer meets your needs and also clarify what additional information would be beneficial at this point. Turning to friends and community members at this stage in the process can also be illuminating.

Revisit Your Must-Haves and Deal Breakers

Knowing the order of importance for your must-haves and deal breakers can be a North Star as you make your decision. Use the example charts as a guide as you reflect on your job offer.

EXAMPLE: Using must-haves to make a decision		
Must-Haves	**Job Offer Details**	**How It Works for You**
Make at least $75,000.	$70,000 with a full benefits package.	I'm going to ask for $75,000 and see what they say, but if this is their best offer, I'm okay with it because it aligns with my ideal work and feels like a good fit.
A manager who makes time for regular constructive feedback and supports ongoing professional development.	I was told that managers have weekly 1:1 meetings with team members. Also, I get $1,500 for professional development annually.	Based on the questions my potential manager asked me in the interview process, I think she will be someone who provides regular feedback. And I'm excited that I get a professional development budget.
At least three weeks of vacation or enough time to recharge regularly.	The job offer includes twenty days of vacation.	It's in the ballpark and I also get sick time, so I feel satisfied.

EXAMPLE:
Using deal breakers to make a decision

Deal Breakers	Job Offer Details	How It Works for You
Not having autonomy over my work.	Unclear.	I get the sense that I will have autonomy based on what I've learned about decision-making and how work gets done.
A manager who micromanages and undermines me.	Need to confirm.	I'm a little worried that my potential manager might want to check in too often, so I'm going to ask her how often she wants to meet 1:1.
A work environment where I have to be "on" 24/7.	Work hours are officially nine to five "on paper."	It seems like a lot of email takes place in the evening. I need to better understand expectations around being "on."

To analyze your decision fully, once you've completed your own chart, you may find it helpful to rate each must-have and deal breaker on a scale of 1–10, with 10 being a job that most satisfies your specific need. We're hopeful that you're a 7 or above (and ideally an 8, 9, or 10) for each must-have and deal breaker. If you're consistently below a 7, you might need additional information or to readjust your expectations. It could be that the job isn't the right fit for you.

Notes

_____

_____

_____

_____

Get Input from Your Community

If you need additional feedback as you're working through your decision, reach out to one or two friends, a coach, or another trusted member of your community for support. Clarify what input would be helpful to you and also what would not be. For example, do you need more information on the organization to make a decision? Are you looking for validation or do you need additional counsel on negotiating your offer?

Decisions this big, by necessity, require heartfelt conversations at home if you have other people who rely on you. You and your partner, for instance, may be at odds over whether or not to take a job—you might face significant pressure either way. Cathy has held coaching sessions with couples to help them navigate difficult conversations about the decision-making process. You might want to consider working with a professional if you're negotiating with a loved one and need help clarifying and prioritizing each of your needs.

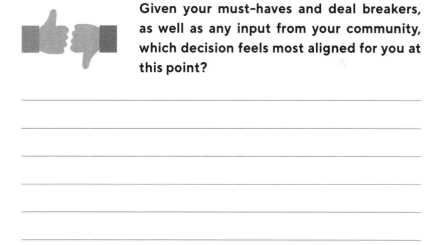 **Given your must-haves and deal breakers, as well as any input from your community, which decision feels most aligned for you at this point?**

One of Cathy's clients, a mid-career management consultant, was recently offered a job. Her partner was excited for her but worried that the salary wasn't high enough. That was a dilemma for Cathy's client, since she was excited about the job and felt okay with the salary, but she also felt pressured by her partner to ask for more money. The couple talked through their shared values and decided that although asking for a higher salary was important, it wasn't a deal breaker. Because of the conversation with her partner, Cathy's client did ask for more money and received a small increase. The fact that the job also met many of her must-haves made it easier for her to make the decision. Even though the salary wasn't ideal, it was sufficient. And by talking about it with her partner, she was able to garner the support she needed to make a decision that felt right for both of them.

Tap into Your Intuition

Now it's time to turn to your *intuition*—an even deeper form of knowing or understanding. Some people think of it as your gut instinct or a higher sense of purpose. The morning and evening practices we've recommended in the book are designed to connect you more deeply to yourself, which builds your intuition. When you're in touch with your intuition, you may simply know what the right decision is even if you can't quite articulate all the reasons why.[16] Getting quiet and into a grounded mindset increases your capacity to listen to your intuition and will help you make a decision.

---

[16] Intuitive decision-making is often unconscious and quite fast compared to a rational decision-making approach. Erik Dane and Michael Pratt. "Exploring Intuition and Its Role in Managerial Decision Making," *The Academy of Management Review*, 32(1), (2007): 33–54. https://doi.org/10.5465/amr.2007.23463682.

Sometimes the best decision is one that doesn't immediately feel completely energizing, but your intuition is telling you it's the right decision in the long term.

 **What do your intuition say is your best decision?**

Make Your Decision

You've worked through a comprehensive decision-making process, which hopefully has revealed important insights for you. If you're feeling energized overall about the job, that's great! Even if an offer isn't exactly what you were hoping for, it might still be the best option for you and your family. Especially in a tough job market, it can be difficult to turn down an offer when you don't have other options. This is a very personal decision, and only you, in consultation with your loved ones, will know what is the best course of action.

 **Now that you've analyzed your decision from multiple angles, what decision best represents the totality of your inner wisdom?**

Prepare to Negotiate

As you've likely heard, when you receive an offer, you have the most leverage. Ideally, you'll receive an offer that feels fair and aligned with your unique value. However, the offer might not be exactly what you want or need. It's understandable to be anxious about asking for more—you may worry about coming across as needy or demanding. We hope that you feel empowered to ask for what you need, though we understand that it can be nerve-racking to do so!

By expressing your needs in the negotiation process, you're continuing to engage in the virtuous cycle and deepening your relationship with your potential employer in an authentic way, building trust and mutuality.

As you negotiate, always do what feels consistent with your values and needs. You want to "go for it," while also being attuned to and respectful of the norms within the organization. For example, it might not be appropriate to negotiate additional time off or ask for a salary that's close to what your manager makes. Read online forums and other reviews and talk to people to validate what is an appropriate salary range and benefits for the role, industry, and/or sector that you're considering, as well as the geographic location.

WHAT'S UP FOR NEGOTIATION?

- Salary
- Bonuses
- Exit agreements
- Promotion schedules
- Flexible work arrangements
- Equity in the company
- Professional development and executive coaching
- Number of vacation days
- Childcare support
- Transportation perks
- Home office and cell phone/internet costs

Even if your potential employer already set expectations in the interviewing process on salary and benefits, you'll want to revisit what you determined is your ideal salary range and benefits in chapter 5. Update your ask based on what you've learned about the position, the organization, and the sector/industry.

Negotiate Effectively

It might be surprising to hear that the best negotiations we've seen usually only last a few minutes and occur within about a week of the initial offer being made.

If possible, you'll want to avoid a process that drags on with multiple conversations about the offer. Do your best to manage the process proactively in a way that feels healthy and appropriate! And be mindful of how you communicate, considering both your own tone and timing and that of your potential employer.

During the actual negotiation conversation, allow for silence so you give the other person space to process what you're sharing. Pay attention to your own feelings and needs and what the other person is expressing. Do your best to communicate in a matter-of-fact and pleasant way, highlighting the facts and try not to get carried away by your emotions. We know this is easier said than done.

Before you head into the conversation, practice with a friend, loved one, coach, or even in front of the mirror! Get clear on what you might say if there's any resistance to the points you're making, without being defensive or going into "selling yourself" mode. That's likely to backfire and move you away from your power.

In the example conversation below, the job seeker has determined that salary is the most important factor for him and is seeking to negotiate a $65K offer. Ideally, he would like $80K. While his deal breaker is $72K, he's hoping that the organization will offer $75K.

KICK OFF THE CONVERSATION

Example Conversation	What to Do	What <u>Not</u> to Do
"I'm thrilled about the opportunity."	Start with authentic gratitude.	Go straight into negotiating.
"I'm particularly excited about the role (be specific about some of what you're hoping to accomplish in the job) and using my skills and experience (be specific again)."	Reinforce your unique value and how you want to create together.	Try to convince your potential employer of your worth.
"I would like to talk through a few questions I have around salary, benefits, and flexibility in the work schedule. Should we start with salary?"	Be as honest and transparent as possible. Queue up the different priorities that you want to negotiate.	Lead with your frustration and disappointment over the offer.

MAKE THE ASK
Ask Directly

Example Conversation	What to Do	What <u>Not</u> to Do
"You offered me $65K, but in order to take this job, I need to make closer to $80K."	Briefly share the reality of what you truly need to accept the position, knowing that there will likely be some negotiation.	Justify why you need this salary, sharing too much information about your personal situation.

Explain Your Limitations and Needs

Example Conversation	What to Do	What **Not** to Do
"It would be really difficult for me to take this job at $65K, as I was making 20 percent more in my last position. Would you be willing to consider a salary closer to $80K?" *(Pause and wait for a response.)*	Help your potential employer understand what your needs are. In this context, it's okay to mention that the offer is lower than what you may have been previously making, ideally expressing the percentage change (as opposed to the actual dollar amount).	Justify why you need this salary because you made more in a previous position.

Highlight Your Market Value

Example Conversation	What to Do	What **Not** to Do
"Based on my research, the average salary for this type of position is $75K. Is there any way that you can increase the salary?" *(Pause and wait for a response.)*	Acknowledge your needs, while bringing in market research and supporting data in a matter-of-fact way.	Get defensive about why you should be earning more based on the market rate and challenge the organization in a way that feels like you're overstepping.

Acknowledge an Employer's Limitations

Example Conversation	What to Do	What **Not** to Do
"I am hoping for close to $80K. I know it's a leap, and it would mean a lot to me if you would be willing to increase the salary." *(Pause and wait for a response.)*	Acknowledge and respect any limitations that your employer might have, while still asking for what you need.	Disregard the limitations your employer has and just ask for what you need.

NEGOTIATE THE OFFER

Accept the Offer

Example Conversation	What to Do	What Not to Do
"Thank you so much for your willingness to consider my requests. I'm excited to say that I would love to formally accept the position."	Reiterate your gratitude and share your enthusiasm for the position.	Forget to share your gratitude in the heat of the moment. Start to get into specific details of the position.

Decline the Offer

Example Conversation	What to Do	What Not to Do
"I'm so grateful for this opportunity, but unfortunately it's not going to work."	After you've had a discussion, either in the moment or afterward, share your gratitude and politely decline the offer. Consider how you might authentically stay in touch, if anything changes in the future.	End the negotiation abruptly. Be openly disappointed or frustrated in a way that damages your relationship with the organization.

You Need More Time to Think it Over

Example Conversation	What to Do	What Not to Do
"Thank you for all the information. It's a lot to consider. I would like to take a few days to think it over. Would that work for you?"	Make sure that you've discussed everything that you want to negotiate. Reiterate your gratitude and ask for more time, if you need it.	Express your disappointment in a way that jeopardizes your integrity or potential role.

WRAP UP THE CONVERSATION

Example Conversation	What to Do	What **Not** to Do
"Let me know how we can best stay in touch over the next few weeks."	Understand the timeline and next steps. If you've accepted the offer, get clear on what's expected before you start.	Forget to ask about the timing and next steps or pressure them to answer you right away.

When possible, discuss the offer over the phone or in person, as tone and nuance can be more difficult to convey via email. Bear in mind that anything you write could be shared within the organization. Additionally, if the organization updates the offer, it's critical to ask for it in writing.

WEIGHING MULTIPLE OFFERS

We believe that in the new work paradigm, it's important to contribute to a more open and transparent negotiation. You shouldn't have to dangle another offer in front of an employer in order to negotiate. However, you will want to mention that you have another offer you're considering, if it's impacting your timeline to make a decision.

If you have a better offer that you're leaning toward, but you aren't as excited about it, it's appropriate to share as a point of discussion, not as a way to convince or entice. For example, some of our clients have used straightforward language: *"I have another offer that I'm leaning toward because it's a higher salary, but I would really prefer to take this position if we can get into more alignment."*

Celebrate AND MAINTAIN MOMENTUM

CONGRATULATIONS! You've worked hard to make an intentional and thoughtful decision. Celebrate by doing something fabulous, you deserve it! You now have a decision-making framework that you can call on for small and large decisions once you start your new job, accessing the totality of your inner wisdom from day one.

Chapter 10

LIVE THE NEW WORK PARADIGM IN YOUR JOB

Get into an <u>OPEN</u> mindset

Build self-awareness at work

Hone your daily schedule

Tap into your unique value

Live out your ideal work

Embrace the Virtuous Cycle

Keep your materials up-to-date

Revolutionize recruitment

Use your inner wisdom to make decisions

Celebrate and maintain momentum

Andrea
BUILDS A HAPPY TEAM

Can't say I wasn't warned, Andrea thought to herself. It had been just a few weeks since she had taken a prominent job as communications director at a well-known international nonprofit.

She knew what she was getting into based on what she'd learned during the interview process, but she had decided to accept the position anyway because the organization's mission strongly resonated with her, and she felt like it was a dream role. And while she liked many aspects of her job and the team she led, there was no denying that it was a toxic workplace, living up to its reputation of being a pressure cooker.

The dysfunctional culture came directly from the CEO, who expected long work hours and set aggressive deadlines and unrealistic performance goals. As a result, many managers perpetuated this culture and staff felt burned out. Yet Andrea wanted to try to do what she could to create a safe haven for her team. She engaged Cathy for leadership coaching to help her.

As she worked with Cathy on the Emotional Breakthrough Process, she started to use it with her team. Checking in with staff, Andrea asked them to name the causes of their stress and anxiety, acknowledging the toll the work environment was taking on each of them. In staff meetings, Andrea asked her staff what they needed and she gave plenty of positive feedback, modeling the thoughtful culture she wanted to build.

It's not easy to counter an organization's culture. But Andrea felt small wins when her team shared how much they appreciated her commitment to creating a safe space to share their feelings and needs, while also driving toward ambitious goals. The result was a happier, more productive team who enjoyed their manager. In fact, other teams started to approach Andrea to get ideas for how to modify some of the negative behaviors they had noticed on their teams and in the organization.

Take a deep breath—we hope that you're feeling excited. We wish we could say the work is done now that you have a new job.

Luckily, the skills you've built looking for a job are the same ones you'll need to excel in your new role.

Whether or not you're a manager like Andrea, if you've done the work in this book, you're likely to begin your job feeling empowered, clear on your unique value, and ready to make lasting contributions.

In this chapter, we not only share ways to set yourself up for success in your new role, but we also encourage you to pay it forward and envision a new work paradigm that is more compassionate, creative, and equitable. Advocating for yourself and others—on everything from salary to professional development—ripples out into the world and creates a more equitable work environment that makes work life better for everyone.

Think about the role you want to play ensuring fair practices and making room for everyone to share their perspective and live out their unique value. How will what you've learned in this book influence the way that you relate to yourself and your colleagues?

By tapping into your feelings and needs and working with the Emotional Breakthrough Process, you're already making a significant contribution. And, when you do this at work, you'll contribute to building more self-aware teams.

As we've discussed throughout the book, power differentials are still prevalent at work and in our broader world. It will require deep and ongoing effort to change these dynamics, and it can be harder when you're early in your career, have limited financial or other resources, or if you've been marginalized.

You may feel that you don't have the ability to impact your teammates and the organizational culture. And yet, as we propose in this book, no matter where you are in your professional journey, you have an opportunity and even a responsibility to live the virtuous cycle, by continuing to empower yourself and support others to do the same, when you can.

Get into an <u>OPEN</u> Mindset

Throughout the book, we've delineated distinct mindsets to help you access different parts of yourself, but in reality, these mindsets are highly interconnected. They serve as tools to help you get present with your feelings, needs, and beliefs.[17] We hope you can tap into the exercises in this book and mindsets going forward.

When you're starting a new job, it's common to feel overwhelmed and sometimes even intimidated. An open mindset helps you to shift your focus outside of yourself, giving you space to discover and experience your new workplace. Imagine yourself as an organizational anthropologist who is looking to understand your new colleagues and the organization's culture and norms. And try to be a sponge: soak in information with as little judgment as possible. This will allow you to be less self-conscious and more available to listen and learn from those around you, laying a solid foundation to have meaningful, productive, and creative relationships.

When Lauren started her most recent job, she asked a number of colleagues in the first few months, *"What advice do you have for me in my new role?"* so she could stay open to new ideas and information. This approach doesn't work for everyone, but in her case, Lauren was able to quickly learn about team dynamics and insights about the organization that were helpful to her role.

---

17 A research study with 129 medical sales employees showed the direct link between mindset and both performance on the job and an employee's relationship with managers. A "growth" mindset, the belief that you can learn and grow through hard work and effort, combined with a manager's strong learning goal orientation, meant better employee-manager relationships overall. Matt Zingoni and Christy Corey, "How Mindset Matters: The Direct and Indirect Effects of Employees' Mindsets on Job Performance," *Journal of Personnel Psychology*, 16(1), (2017): 1-10, https://doi.org/10.1027/1866-5888/a000171.

Another idea is to develop a new morning mantra to serve as a compass for your job such as, *"I bring an open mind and commit to being available to new experiences and contribute to shaping the workplace I want to work in."*

How will you stay in an open mindset in your new job?

Build Self-Awareness at Work

Imagine if more workplaces created appropriate ways to process how you're feeling, what you need to do your best work, and what beliefs may be limiting you.

When you take stock of your feelings and needs, you're much more likely to stay attuned to yourself, giving you the space to engage thoughtfully with others. This allows you to be in the virtuous cycle, increasing the likelihood that you can create together with more freedom and ease.

Some organizations are already creating dedicated positions that focus on well-being. We hope that *"VP of Mindset"* or *Chief Emotional Officer* (the new CEO!) becomes commonplace in the future! You can do your part by sharing what you do to work with your emotions and stay connected to your power—that will help normalize and build community around it.

Recently, at Lauren's company, an employee resource group was created to focus on employees' mental health. This has opened up more conversation around well-being and brought emotions to the forefront. While not every employee is involved in the group, it's created a conversation within the company about what it means to share feelings and needs—and the company now has wellness days. Initiatives like these can have larger impacts in the organization and the world.

The more feelings and needs are part of the conversation at work—dare we say—the more organizations can solve the many pressing issues that we face as a world today.

 Call to Action: Ask for regular feedback

In the workplace, one of the best ways to build your self-awareness is to ask for regular (weekly or bi-monthly) feedback that speaks to both your strengths and areas for development. This is a perfect opportunity for you to expand on your unique value, while being cognizant of your feelings and needs. We suggest that you consider the *front door formula*, clarifying what type of feedback you're looking for and how you will process it (hint, hint, the Emotional Breakthrough Process will likely come in handy!).

Hone Your Daily Schedule

Imagine if you and your colleagues had an inspiring workload that was also manageable. And a flexible meeting schedule that you could adjust based on your working style and how, where, and how much you want to work. We think this approach to work would result in people feeling more fulfilled and at ease, and likely more productive and capable of doing their best.

As you settle into your role, give yourself enough time to identify how you can optimize your work-rest cycle and daily schedule. You'll need to figure out what works within your routine and be intentional about how you fit everything in.

Ask yourself such questions as:
- What have I learned about my optimal work-rest cycle from my job search?
- How am I going to prioritize my work and stay productive and also take care of myself while getting the rest and renewal that I need?
- How much time should I dedicate to my email and other communications?

- How often do I want to check in with my manager and my team?
- How am I going to stay motivated and make sure I'm on track with major projects?

It can be challenging to make time for your morning and evening practice, but doing so can be transformative during your first few months and help you stay grounded in your power.

Additional practices that will serve you well:
- **Bite-size your work:** Consider organizing your workload into discrete, doable tasks, while still building in time for deep work sessions.
- **Create buffer time:** Structure breaks or buffer time between meetings so you can reenergize and rejuvenate. Build in more time than you think you need.
- **Manage your to do list:** Prioritize what you need to do daily. Calibrate that list with your manager and those around you, without losing sight of your goals.
- **Plan for unexpected projects and distractions:** Factor in time for unexpected opportunities and challenges. Also, develop strategies for how you'll manage obligations and distractions at work and home.
- **Celebrate your wins:** Regularly take stock of your successes. Make time to recognize what you've been able to accomplish!

MANAGE MEETING FATIGUE

Be honest with yourself about your capacity for meetings. Consider how you could spend less than half your day in meetings and at least one day where you have large chunks of time without meetings. Discern what meetings you can say no to. Increasingly, more organizations are dedicating Fridays or specific periods of time as off-limits for meetings. Start a conversation with your manager and team to improve the meeting culture where you work.

Call to Action: Be explicit about your work style and schedule

We encourage you to proactively share as much as you feel comfortable with what you need to do your best work and ask others what they need as well. Be explicit about what your preferences are with your manager and your team given your optimal work-rest cycle and work style. When you do so, you set a far-reaching example for your colleagues.

Tap into Your Unique Value

Imagine if everyone knew that they had a unique value—including both strengths and vulnerabilities—and expressed it more fully at work. Doing so would help you and your colleagues tap into your collective wisdom and create the space for others to do the same.

Engaging with each other around your unique values will help you get to know each other on a deeper level, providing you with more resources to problem-solve and find solutions together. You are able to share both your strengths and vulnerabilities, normalizing the reality of being human. When you and your colleagues recognize each other's unique value, you're able to collaborate more effectively, decrease conflict and support each other in meaningful ways. This is a key example of the virtuous cycle at work!

 ### *Call to Action:* Start a conversation about your unique value

Just by using the terminology "unique value," you can help catalyze a conversation about your strengths and vulnerabilities, and build stronger relationships. For example, if you feel comfortable, let your manager and/or team know about the work you've done on your unique value and how you express it at work.

You might decide to put together a 1 – 2 page "user manual" that highlights a few aspects of your unique value to help your colleagues work with you better. Ask them to do the same.

Live Out Your Ideal Work

Imagine if more people were doing work they were most interested in that aligned with their values and vision. We think people would likely be happier and organizations would be more productive and fun!

Regularly remind yourself what you want most in your work and revisit your must-haves and deal breakers. Use the chart below to take stock of what's working and what isn't in your new job.

3–6 MONTH CHECK-IN		
	WHAT IS AND ISN'T ALIGNED FOR YOU?	WHAT SHIFTS, IF ANY, DO YOU WANT TO EXPLORE?
Your specific role or job function		
Organizational culture, structure, and decision-making		
Your relationship with your manager		
How you're working with your colleagues and team		
Professional development and learning		

Call to Action: **Move toward your ideal work**

As you start to realize what is and isn't working for you in your new job, prioritize one to two aspects that you might want to shift, if any. Check in with your manager to start a conversation on how you might tweak aspects of your role. As you do this, you might also discover that you could help fix underlying organizational issues such as meeting structure or communication. Consult your Inspiration and Advisory Board and/or close community members you decide on the timing and how to approach these conversations, and in the meantime, build on what you think is working.

Embrace the Virtuous Cycle

Imagine if we lived in a world where everyone understood and valued the virtuous cycle, taking responsibility for their feelings and needs and inviting others to do the same. In this new paradigm, we would have connected conversations that bring us closer together, despite our differences.

Living in the virtuous cycle and having meaningful conversations helps people feel safer, more connected, and more confident, opening up new ways of collaborating and solving the serious challenges we face as a society. When you're truly in the virtuous cycle, you'll notice that you have to slow down regularly in order to be empowered and more available to yourself and others.

To help you navigate the first few months of your new job (and beyond), consider having a formal accountability partner, whether it's a friend or a coach. And we hope that your Inspiration and Advisory Board can continue to serve as a guidepost for you! Community building is a lifelong process. Continue having connected conversations to learn about the people in your workplace and industry, while developing ongoing talking points to advocate for ideas and projects.

***Call to Action:* Check in with your community**

In your first few months, think about your support team and how they helped you navigate the search. Consider updating them on your new job and thanking them again! Reflect on your own power in your new position. How are you being intentional about living out the virtuous cycle and having connected conversations that help you—and others?

Keep Your Materials Up-to-Date

Imagine if your application materials never got old. That is, you constantly updated your professional accomplishments and contributed to your workplace in a way that built your skills and your portfolio for your next role. It's easy to think that once you get a job; you can stop paying attention to your online presence and application materials. But that's not the case—you'll want to update your LinkedIn profile and keep an up-to-date bio and résumé so you're always in the mode of sharing your unique value and ideal work; in doing so, you invite others to do the same.

Toward that end, update your résumé a couple of times a year. It might be most helpful to keep your back-office résumé up to date too, so you can keep track of all of your successes. We also encourage you to draw on all of the work that you did on your cover letters and any work proposals that you wrote during your job search as templates to pitch new ideas and projects, as you gather support for specific initiatives. These documents are more similar than you might think!

 ***Call to Action:* Update your LinkedIn profile and résumé**

Now that you have a new position, update your LinkedIn profile, and if you're feeling energized, post what you've learned about the job search and yourself in the process (tag this book if you are feeling inspired or write a review)! While you might not want to look at your résumé again for a while, take a pass at adding a few bullets that you can revisit when you're a few months into your job.

Revolutionize Recruitment

Imagine if hiring felt truly mutual and rooted in the virtuous cycle. Both applicants and hiring managers would share their unique value, including vulnerabilities, to discern fit. Organizations would need to relinquish some power by sharing more of how they actually function upfront, such as the reality of their culture and values. Job seekers and employers would have more accurate information to make a good decision that better reflects their needs and goals, building a collaborative, equitable and humane workplace.

Take every opportunity to humanize the recruitment experience. As you write job descriptions, be realistic about the workload for the position, accounting for the time it will take to manage staff, administrative activities and unexpected work. Include a timeline for the hiring process and be as explicit as you can be with the salary range. When you're interviewing, take the time to really get to know applicants and even work with them for an afternoon or a few days if possible.

Make a commitment to be proactive and responsive as you keep potential candidates in the loop, updating them on where they stand and what the next steps are. If you've interviewed a candidate who isn't moving forward in the process, send a personalized email or call. Avoid sending generic emails. And of course, please don't ghost candidates. When you can, offer to share feedback. Ultimately, revolutionizing recruitment will equalize the playing field and empower both job seekers and organizations.

Call to Action: **Shape the Recruitment Process**

Soon enough, you'll likely be a decision maker in your organization, if you aren't already. Think about the role you want to play in ensuring fair practices and making room for everyone to share their perspective and live out their unique value. How will you commit to challenging the power dynamic in hiring processes? How will you ensure that the process is as humane as possible? How will you stay mindful of your biases as you make decisions about who to hire?

Use Your Inner Wisdom to Make Decisions

No matter your title, you'll make dozens of decisions every day on the job—from scheduling meetings to deciding who you want to include on a project team. Imagine if you're so dialed into your values and what guides your decision-making (rational, emotional, intuitive) that you have a clear sense of how to prioritize your work. And other people look to you because they recognize your ability to identify "true north," whether it's a new strategy, program, or process that you're revamping. People get behind you and your ideas.

Take the following steps to keep building your decision-making prowess on the job:

✔ Consider how your values inform your decisions.
✔ Get all the information you need on the decisions you're making.
✔ What authority and/or autonomy do you have to make the decision?
✔ Who needs to be involved in the decision? (And who will be bothered if they aren't included in the process?)
✔ How will you use decision-making to build relationships with the people you work with and more fully enter into the virtuous cycle?

Once you've made a few big decisions at work, ask yourself:

✔ What have you learned about yourself, your manager, your team, and the organization by making this decision? How did it go? And what would you do differently?

✔ How will what you've learned inform how you make decisions in the future?

✔ How do you want to celebrate your decision?

 ### *Call to Action:* Share your decision-making process

Helping make what often is implicit, explicit can help build connection and resolve conflict and misunderstanding at work. Consider sharing your decision-making process with others and ask them about theirs—so you can better understand how decisions are made. This will help you enter the virtuous cycle more deeply, which can be particularly useful when you're in the middle of a difficult decision.

We hope that you're inspired to not only empower yourself in your job search, but also to continually deepen your power and contribute meaningfully in your new job. Ultimately, we hope that you're energized to build a more compassionate, creative, and equitable workplace and world!

About the Book

In 2016, through an introduction from a mutual professional colleague, Cathy and Lauren met over tea on a wintry day in New York City across from Bryant Park. We discovered that we share a passion for inspiring personal and professional growth in others, poetry, and Frida Kahlo!

Cathy had been coaching individuals, teams, and organizations for over twenty years and saw the critical importance of working with clients' emotions. Over the years, she created many strategies to help her clients navigate their emotions at work and in the job search to own their power.

As a leadership and career coach, Lauren recognized the need to bring job seekers together to make the job search less lonely and isolating. When she went on to lead hiring processes at a search firm, she had a front-row seat at the often grueling process of finding a job, and how unfair it sometimes felt.

Shortly after we met, we joined forces to co-create *CareerLeap*, a career leadership program for the Charles and Lynn Schusterman Family Foundation, where Lauren worked at the time. CareerLeap brought job seekers together to help them navigate their job search and develop leadership skills. The more we collaborated, the more we realized that we shared a similar vision: when people feel empowered to work with the full range of their emotions, they can build a more compassionate, creative, and equitable work world.

In the process of writing this book, Lauren went through two job transitions herself. When COVID hit, she was furloughed and decided to look for a new job. She embraced the practices she and Cathy were writing about. Applying for jobs in the middle of a global pandemic required her to stay optimistic, focus on her mindset, and set up daily routines to stay grounded and disciplined. She landed a great job.

When we started writing this book, we set out on a mission to help job seekers connect to their own sense of power and build a better work world. Who would have imagined the social, political, health, and environmental turmoil that 2020 would bring? The tumultuous and tragic year made us rethink the book and recommit to helping more people deal with emotional challenges as they look for a new job.

We hope our book has helped you! Let us know and share your story by tagging #theempoweredjobsearch on social media, writing a review online and/or sending us an email at theempoweredjobsearch@gmail.com.

Our website is **theempoweredjobsearch.com**.

Acknowledgments

Cathy: I want to thank the hundreds of wonderful clients I've had over more than twenty years. You have entrusted me to partner with you on the journey of finding great work and more deeply accessing and sharing your power and gifts! I've learned so much from you and I'm incredibly grateful.

Thank you to Russ Finkelstein, Ami Dar and Lea Policoff who asked me to write 'Ask Cathy,' my career column for Idealist in 2000. Your request inspired me to do this work so I'm very grateful for the nudge to fulfill part of my professional destiny.

A huge thank you to my dear colleague Lauren Weinstein for being such an amazing, smart, and fun collaborator. We wrote every sentence of the book together and did so with ease, humor and a sense of discovery and purpose. A big thank you too to Lauren's husband, Eli Kintisch for being such a big supporter of this book and a great editor/writer and thought partner with us.

My friends are numerous and to each of you, I say a big thank you, especially to Ann Lordeman and Janet Waterston for their ongoing encouragement and interest in the book. A deep thank you to Trisha Hoffman for supporting me in my work to continue to discover my own power. And to Elaine and Roland Gyllenhammer who supported me so deeply in my journey over many decades, you are always with me.

A big thank you to my nieces and nephews for being such an inspiration, I love you all very much—Amanda Wasserman, Kurt Wasserman, Rebecca Wasserman, Raquel Wasserman, Alec Wasserman, and David Wasserman, may you always feel supported, loved and fully engaged by your work and life!

Thank you to Maren Masino, Emily Levin, and Elliot Zeisel for your guidance and reminders of my power and unique value.

Thank you to Hannah Lindenbaum for helping us write the first draft of the book with her keen insight. And much gratitude to Alieza Durana for her editing and bright and gentle support throughout the process.

Thank you too to my Inspirational Advisory Board, particularly James Baldwin who remains one of the world's biggest beacons of truth ever, Frida Kahlo whose art revealed the interior of her own heart's joy and suffering in such a gorgeous way, Charles Blow who is a modern day seer and truth speaker that we need more than ever, and the great Virginia Woolf who laid a large part of the foundation for my understanding of power.

I also recognize the experiences that have taught me about the shadow side of power. I have learned much from closely examining what can go wrong with individuals, organizations and society when power is out of balance, particularly with covert narcissism.

Lastly, but in no way least, mountains of gratitude and love to all of the wild animals who fill my world with so much joy and wonder. Thank you for deepening my awakening to the sublime and authentic power of the natural world. I am forever in awe and delight!

Lauren: In the process of writing this book, I gave birth to my beloved son, Nadav, started graduate school, and made two job transitions. A huge thank you to my husband, Eli Kintisch. I am eternally grateful for all your help on the book and at home—I couldn't have done it without you. Now it's your turn to pursue your creative pursuits!

Thank you to my dear friend and co-author Cathy for believing in this project. What a journey! I've learned so much from you and am grateful for your commitment to the book, your partnership, sense of humor and friendship.

I want to thank Hannah Lindenbaum and Alieza Durana for helping us conceptualize and edit the book in its early stages. Also, heartfelt gratitude for Alice Kintisch for her edits. I'm grateful for various family, friends, and professional contacts who provided feedback and insights at different stages of the process: Shelley Danner, Adam Fagen, Josh Feldman, Isabel Friedenzohn, Jenna Gebel, Dan Gordon, Elana Hoffman, Avi Kumin, Sandra Marks, Lilah Pomerance, Adam Smiley Poswolsky, Megan Schumann, and Anthony Shop.

To the warm and nurturing incredible caretakers who have helped our family: Lisa Apple, Sterling Jarrett, and the David Star's Family: Yaneth Arias, Daniel Arias, Karen Elias, Paola Machado, Maria Leticia Naranjo, Jessenia Rodriguez, Blanca Soto, and Jessenia Vanegas. I wrote part of this book during COVID and I am grateful for my neighborhood friends who made life more manageable and fun: Kara Kroes Li, Loren Heinbach, Sophie Welter and Emily Wexler.

I would not be here without the thoughtful mentors who have supported me during my career and the extensive opportunities I've had along the way. Mrim Boutla, a brilliant mentor and friend, introduced me to career coaching. To my StartingBloc ladies—Megan Schumann, Erica Schlaikjer, Katrina Gordon, Anna Schumacher, and Shelley Danner—thanks for your encouragement and friendship during this time. To my PennCLO community: Thank you for your wisdom: Annie McKee, Nigel Paine, Kandi Wiens and the Hashtag cohort. Also, to my Degreed colleagues: I learn so much from you every day.

Thank you to my dear friends and family: Ashley Berger, Lisa Bonos, Leemor Chandally, Aryn Fleegler, Annie Frome, Noah

Karesh, Yael Kiken, Ben Kintisch, Stefanie Ginsburg, Danielle Hardoon, Lee Jacobs, Mike Masserman, Sarah Waxman, Brad Weinstein and Paul Weinstein for your ongoing love and support. To my parents, Gary and Lois, for always believing in me and encouraging me to dream even bigger. This can-do mindset has inspired me throughout my life and has shaped me. You have given me so much.

About the Authors

Cathy Wasserman

Cathy is a leadership coach, organization development consultant, licensed master social worker, and 'social experimentrice' dedicated to re-imagining what's possible for individuals, organizations and society. For more than 20 years, she has helped hundreds of people develop their leadership and manifest their ideas — from CEO's to activists, artists to non-profit professionals, and social entrepreneurs. She also advises nonprofits, start-ups, and fellowships including Roddenberry, Schusterman and Wexner. Additionally, she facilitates staff retreats, game-changing conversations, workshops and conflict mediation.

Cathy brings a deep background in community organizing, youth programming and management consulting. Her writing is included in *Frontline Feminism, Sh'ma: A Journal of Jewish Responsibility* and she wrote the 'Ask Cathy' column for Idealist. org. She also has been featured as an expert in The Washington Post, Working Mother magazine, *Super Girls Speak Out* and in the *Idealist Guide to Nonprofit Careers*.

Cathy has an MSW from Smith College and a BA in Psychology from Wesleyan University. She trained in mediation with the New York Peace Institute and in Marshall Rosenberg's Nonviolent Communication. A committed meditator for over 20 years, Cathy has lived on an ashram, an experience, which taught her a great deal about self-empowerment. She has taken regular sabbaticals to travel the world, visiting more than 40 countries. She is also an artist who writes poetry and creates what she calls 'social installations,' integrating writing, visual art, community building and social change. Her first book, *On Rendering Heartbreak Obsolete,* was published in 2004. More about her work can be found at **cathywasserman.com**.

Lauren Weinstein

Lauren has spent over a decade helping hundreds of people navigate their professional career paths and working with organizations to make them healthy and productive. She leads internal learning and development at Degreed, a learning and upskilling platform. Previously, at Raffa-Marcum, she created leadership development offerings and worked with boards to hire, coach, and advise executives in the nonprofit and social sector. Prior roles include running CareerHub, a technology platform / job board for job seekers, at the Charles and Lynn Schusterman Family Foundation and seven years at Accenture as a management consultant.

Lauren received a BA in Communication from the University of Pennsylvania, where she is currently doing an executive master's and doctoral program in organizational leadership and learning. A former competitive swimmer, Lauren has a certification in leadership coaching from Georgetown University and is an Associate Certified Coach (ACC) through the International Coach Federation.

In 2014, Lauren wrote *Coaching is Calling: A Guide to Coach Training Programs and Professional Career Paths*. She lives in Washington, DC, with her husband and adorable toddler. You can find out more at **laurenbweinstein.com**.

Made in the USA
Columbia, SC
23 June 2021